We Owe It To Ourselves
ED ANGER

BY JIMINEY!

WE OWE IT TO OURSELVES!

I may be madder than a cat with kitty litter between his toes, but I'm not too mad to do something about it.

Me and my beer-drinking buddies, Larry Eblin and Alan Perry, were pounding a few at the Lamp Post Grill after work recently, when some pencil-neck walks in and asks for change for the parking meter.

Python, the bartender, says, "Sure, are ya drinkin' here?" And the little toad says, "No, I'm going to the animal rights rally across the street."

Python reaches over the bar and grabs him, folds him up, and mails him in the postbox outside. It's the kind of thing that makes that metal plate in my head hotter than molten lava. We're losing our rights at a rate of three a week these days to criminals, aliens, and screaming, bleeding-heart liberals, and it's time to take a stand. To borrow the slogan from my thwarted 1992 presidential campaign, WE OWE IT TO OURSELVES.

Take this whole "Contract with America" thing, for instance. Now don't get me wrong—I love Newt. He's a big, burly man's man who got up to bat and hit it out of the park. And that makes him A-okay in my book. But I'm thinking Newt hasn't gone far enough and I'll tell you why.

Reason #1: Contracts smell like lawyers and we don't need to get into any lawyerly situations if we don't have to. Reason #2: What's so magic about 100 days? The cures I like for what ails us are fast-acting, big old power-punches that really do the trick—if we don't see results within 48 hours we're barking up the wrong tree. Reason #3: Unfortunately, the America Newt's talking about in his contract is some kind of mirage on a hot highway. My America, the millions of hard-working, tax-paying, television-watching citizens that read my column every single week, are the ones who've been robbed at gunpoint of the American dream. No lunkheaded government plan is going to give them back their piece of the pie. We need real solutions that work—and FAST. I've got my own contract, a contract with *my* America, that I think's just what the doctor ordered.

And what about all the other nonsense, the what-the-hell's-wrong-with-this-country stuff I'm forced to write about every week, just as a public service? President Clinton and her husband Bill, for instance. Now she makes me pig-biting mad, marching around pretending she isn't sitting there with her big feet on the desk in the Oval Office every day, running this country into the ground while Bill's chasing skirts around the reflecting pool. And that daughter they've got! Why are Democrats' daughters so ugly?

Listen, I'm not America's favorite columnist for nothing. I know what makes me mad and I'm not afraid to pipe up about it. I get thousands of letters from angry readers every week, all of them saying, "We're mad, too, by God. You're shooting straight, Ed, so tell 'em how to fix it." This book's for all of us—WE OWE IT TO OURSELVES.

Ed Anger

LET'S PAVE THE STUPID RAINFORESTS & GIVE SCHOOL TEACHERS STUN GUNS

AND other ways to save America

by *Ed Anger*

A Seth Godin Production

BROADWAY BOOKS New York

To Dodger and Blossom

All photographs courtesy of *Weekly World News* and American Media, Inc.

Broadway Books titles may be purchased for business or promotional use
or for special sales. For information, please write to: Special Markets
Department, Bantam Doubleday Dell Publishing Group, Inc., 1540
Broadway, New York, NY 10036.

BROADWAY BOOKS and its logo, a letter B bisected on the diagonal, are
trademarks of Broadway Books, a division of Bantam Doubleday Dell
Publishing Group, Inc.

FIRST EDITION

Designed by Karen Engelmann

ISBN 0-553-06685-4

96 97 98 99 00 10 9 8 7 6 5 4 3 2 1

CONTENTS

 Inside!

IT'S TIME TO PUT AMERICA'S FAVORITE COLUMNIST IN THE WHITE HOUSE!

Every Presidential candidate worth a plug nickel knows you have to have fire in the belly, guts of steel, and a will of iron to make the big run—and maybe a head made of wood, by gum.

I swore after the 1992 campaign I'd never get into that racket again—my wife Thelma Jean is still taking tranquilizers over the bikini shot of my lard-butt daughter-in-law Candy that ran in all the papers.

But I can't ignore the sacks full of mail I get every week begging me to take this country by the reins and get it back on track.

So if you're as sick as I am of all the liberal pabulum Bill and Hillary have been dishing out, you'll stand up right now, wherever you are, and yell at the top of your lungs—ED ANGER FOR PRESIDENT! And as this battle cry of freedom rings out across

Help send Ed Anger to the White House! Clip this button and tape it to your car window. Make copies and give them to your friends!

THE CONTRACT WITH MY AMERICA

ED ANGER FOR PRESIDENT!

this great land, there will be no doubt about it—Mr. and Mrs. Joe Public are mad as hell and they aren't going to take it anymore, by golly.

We're tired of pimply-faced punks shooting our brave policemen and getting away with it because they're "children."

We're tired of watching millions of shiftless aliens flood our shores and drain our country dry.

We're tired of creeps who got AIDS by practicing kinky sex or shooting heroin taking up every bed in our hospitals, leaving no room for people with normal American diseases.

We're tired of foreigners in our cities who jabber in every language BUT English.

We're tired of lawyers breeding like flies and helping themselves to double portions of the American pie every chance they get.

And we're tired of traitors bringing stupid, sissy games like World Cup soccer to this great country, luring our children away from real men's games like football.

Yes, America is fed up. So I've decided to share my Rx for this once great country and let the good American people decide who should be living at 1600 Pennsylvania Avenue.

THE CONTRACT WITH MY AMERICA

The five principles of my basic philosophy of American civilization go like this:

- **Smoking anywhere, anytime, is a Constitutional right.**

- **Real justice hurts.**

- **A gun in every holster.**

- **A fresh credit slate for every American man, woman, and child.**

- **Buy American.**

The Contract With My America I've dreamed up is so simple I'm amazed no one's thought of it before. This scheme calls for swift and decisive passage of the following ten pieces of legislation—and I'm offering a money-back guarantee that these laws will make America great again:

THE JUDGE ROY BEAN MEMORIAL CRIME AND PUNISHMENT ACT

Named for the late great promoter of pure pistol justice, this is a surefire recipe for a crime-free America:

The People's Court Plank

- Any criminal committing a second offense for anything would not be entitled to a lawyer but would still be allowed a jury trial.

- Any criminal committing a third offense of any kind wouldn't get a lawyer or a jury trial.

- Any criminal committing rape, murder, or child abuse would have their case decided by a hardass judge in his private chambers—with sentence handed down the minute he found the creep guilty as charged.

- Appeals by Death Row inmates would be limited to one paragraph—and the hardass judge would personally give them a thumbs up or a thumbs down.

- All convicts would be allowed just one Supreme Court appeal per lifetime.

The Ed Anger Criminal Justice Revision Plank

- Police officers will be allowed to arrest someone and hold a mini-trial right there on the spot. The criminal would be arrested, tried, and executed within 24 hours without a lot of yackety-yak from lawyers, judges, and other do-gooders, by gum.

- Police officers will be allowed to whip vandals, Singapore Caning Squad-style, right there on the spot, instead of sending them off to the fancy resorts they pass off for prisons nowadays.

The Put-the-Public-Back-in-Public-Television Plank

- Televise executions—give those budding young rapists a taste of what's in store for them. As long as we're doling out money to those bleeding-heart public

television types, we may as well carve out a little prime time for My America. (And no last requests like new Bibles or gourmet meals for these Death Row cockroaches—they've cost us too much already.)

WHY I LIKE THE GUILLOTINE

I'm happier than Michael Jackson at a Cub Scout Jamboree over the new electronic guillotine that will soon replace the gas chamber and lethal injections for executing Death Row creeps in many states. Personally, I like to see these animals fry like slabs of bacon in the electric chair, but this new guillotine sounds great, too.

There's nothing like the sound of a murderer or rapist screaming and crying just before the dull thud of a head being lopped off. I read in a book about the French Revolution that a guillotine victim can look around and think for up to 10 minutes after his noggin has been sliced off. Now that's something I'd like to see.

The gas chamber has always been a wimpy way to kill these human cockroaches and lethal injection is even easier on 'em. Let's give these child molesters and other scum something to think about—like the sight of a razor-sharp, stainless-steel blade coming down on their necks.

Several states—including Arkansas, North Carolina, Texas, and Illinois—are currently considering the switch to the guillotine. And I say, get to it, boys—time's a-wasting.

The Flag-burning Eradication Plank

• For a reasonable fee, any red-blooded American can kick the stuffing out of the fruitcakes who burn or damage the American flag.

ED ANGER'S NEW DEAL

My plan for economic recovery is so simple, I can't believe no one ever came up with it before.

Balance the Budget

I can balance the goldurned budget in one minute flat. I'm getting tired of hearing about it so I say we just wipe the slate clean and give America a fresh start. The deficit will be zero with a stroke of a pen, for crying out loud. What the hell, Brazil has been doing it for years—and belly laughing all the way to the bank.

Tax Chops

Let's cut taxes by 50% immediately. We'll have so much money on payday we'll have to carry it home in grocery bags.

Buy American Or Else

Make it a capital crime to buy ANYTHING that isn't made in America. In other words, traitors who buy Toyotas and Mitsubishi TVs would fry in the chair, by jiminey! Hey, I know these are pretty tough measures. But if we're going to pull ourselves up by the bootstraps, we're going to have to kick some butt. And I fig-ure Japan's a good place to start. I never bought anything Mr. Moto and his buck-toothed buddies have shipped over here to America. But a lot of good-hearted, patriotic Americans have been hoodwinked for years into paying good money for the junk these rice ball racketeers peddle. Well, it's high time

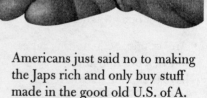

Americans just said no to making the Japs rich and only buy stuff made in the good old U.S. of A.

Turn Big Money into Little Money

This one's a home run, by gum. Every American will trade in each of his regular-size bills for two smaller ones. In other words, you turn in a regular-size $5 bill and you get two smaller $5 bills in return. Double your money, two for one—get it? Every American could double their net worth overnight. And with twice the money to spend, consumers would fuel the biggest economic rebound in American history.

The Three-Income Plan

Let every American man have two wives at once. That'll do it,

ladies and gentlemen. Right there you'll have instant three-income families. Imagine how many big-ticket items you could buy with three paychecks rolling in every week, by golly. And when the kids are sick, the wives could take turns staying home with 'em so the husband wouldn't have to miss any time from his higher-paying job. Just think how many jobs we would create with this blockbuster plan. People would be buying up cars, stoves, and stereos to beat the band. And guess who would be hired to build all this stuff? One of the family's two wives, that's who! Brilliant, huh?

Now, I know all those screeching women's libbers out there are going to pitch a hissy-fit about this plan, but to hell with 'em. They aren't the ones trying to pay the bills and raise kids—because most of them live with other women, if you get my drift.

And if you want a hot stock tip, try bridal gear. When this plan becomes reality, we'll have millions of weddings every year as men marry second wives—or even tie the knot with a couple of them at once. Getting hitched could become America's biggest business.

The Zero Balance Due Scheme

In a bold move, we'll just forgive everybody's debts on Labor Day. Except for home mortgages, of course. That's right, folks. We'll create a fresh credit slate for every man, woman, and child in America! No matter who or what you owe—auto loans, credit cards, finance companies, record clubs—every single loan would have a zero balance come noon on Labor Day. That means you owe goose eggs, nada, nothing—a perfect credit report even if you haven't made a car payment in six months!

People would go spend-crazy for the first time since Ronald Reagan was in office. And you

know what that means? Yep. Jobs, folks. As stuff pours out of the stores at a record clip, factories would shift into high gear to keep the Wal-Mart shelves stocked and cash registers across this great land would be smoking. The only people who would be out of work would be those pesky bill collectors. They wouldn't have anybody to hound about late payments because there wouldn't be any late payments.

THE DUNCE CAP EDUCATION REFORM ACT

First Choice: Bring back the dunce cap, those long pointy cone hats that old-fashioned teachers used to make dumb kids wear. Dumb kids will have to wear the dunce cap so often they'll finally quit school and never have a chance to be stupid in college. By eliminating these bonebrains early, the other kids are able to learn at a much faster pace.

Now, I know those whining liberal bleeding hearts who took over our schools in the 1960s will scream bloody murder. But every teacher should be issued dunce caps to put on stupid kids—and keep them from getting into college and being stupid there, too.

Second Choice: Every public school student from sea to shining sea will wear a National Public School Uniform—white shirts and Bermuda shorts for boys, white blouses with Peter Pan collars and black skirts for girls.

Third Choice: Shut down the public school system in this country right now and put all that tax money where it belongs—into college scholarships for smart kids, not calculators for dimwits.

THE HEARTH AND HOME ENFORCED FAMILY VALUES ACT

Ban breast-feeding in public! Any woman who does it should be arrested and thrown in jail with all the other common criminals, by jiminey. Let's face it. Why ban our kids from X-rated movies when they can see some

Carnegie-Atex ALERT!

Of 30,000 students surveyed at 500 four-year colleges:

- 38% think George Washington is a football player!

- 49% do not know who the President is.

- 20% still think Ronald Reagan is in office.

- A **WHOPPING** 68% of kids questioned said South Carolina was located below Florida on the map.

- A surprising 64% of the female students think women are smarter than men, despite study after study that proves otherwise.

- A **SHOCKING** 91% didn't know Abraham Lincoln invented the potato chip!

- An **AMAZING** 52% of freshmen couldn't subtract 396 from 748 and get anywhere near the right answer. Some said their high school teacher never taught them to subtract big numbers because the teachers themselves didn't know how.

- A **SICKENING** 76% of America's college kids said if they could go anywhere in the world to further their education, they would pick Disney World.

- And the one question that makes me **PIG-BITING MAD**! When asked to name the country that invented the automobile, airplane, baseball, and was the first to land on the moon, 43% answered Japan.

Tell me America's not going to hell in a hand basket if we don't start crackin' some heads in the classrooms across our great land—and **I MEAN NOW**!

breast-feeding fruitcake hanging around the bus stop or strolling through their local mall any day of the week.

Bring back the corset!
Every unmarried gal should wear one to stop the spread of sexual disease and moral degeneration. Teach high school girls how to wear one of these steel and elastic products instead of how to use contraceptives. When it comes to cleaning up the sex mess in America, young women are our only hope.

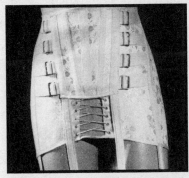

Teach college coeds to be great housewives!
I gotta tell you, folks, things have been going downhill fast ever since women's lib hit the scene back in the 1960s and gals start-ed running around burning their bras and getting jobs on construction crews. It messed up our country so dag-blamed much that it's taken us all this time to recover. Colleges should have courses featuring screenings of the old Donna Reed Show. That show's still the perfect example of how to be a good mother and wife. Give college girls a big dose of Donna Reed the first thing every morning and before you know it we'll have a nation full of happy homemakers baking apple pies and driving the neighborhood kids back and forth to kindergarten.

THE LOCKED DOOR ANTI-IMMIGRATION ACT

Close our borders now. It's that simple.

THE QUALITY OF MY LIFE ENHANCEMENT ACT

Okay, I'll admit this one's all about Numero Uno—that mean's ME, for those of you who don't speak chili pepperese, as we call it here in the Anger family—and

ED ANGER TIME
(OR E.A.T)

I came up with this little tidbit in my spare time—my Ed Anger Time! Instead of just moving the clock ahead one hour for Daylight Savings Time, move the clocks ahead TWO hours. That means when you get off work at 5 o'clock it'll REALLY only be 3 o'clock—and that means nearly six hours of fun 'n' sun AFTER work, folks. That's enough time to play a round of golf, mow the lawn, and still have an hour or two of sun left for fishing—every single day! It's twice as good as Daylight Savings Time!

So let's make it official. On the first Sunday of May, at 2:00 a.m. Eastern Standard Time, move your clocks ahead one MORE hour. You won't believe how long and wonderful those summer afternoons can be till you've experienced them on Ed Anger Time. It's an idea whose time has come.

If these big government worrywarts had their way, all food would be stamped WARNING: EAT THIS AND YOU'LL GET FAT OR DIE. Great! If you're stupid enough to believe that, you DESERVE to starve to death.

WHY CABLE IS A CRIME!

What makes me so pig-biting mad is that I used to love the weather—talkin' about it, predictin' it, or just walking around in it. But now that cable TV put that all-day, all-night Weather Channel on the tube, all the fun's gone. These bozos do NOTHING but talk about the weather every minute of every day and make computer forecasts 10 days in advance.

They've even made the weather boring. My set has an exercise channel, a shopping channel, a religious channel, a sex channel, a science fiction channel, a country channel, and a fishing channel, to name just a few.

What'll they try to plug me into next—a dog grooming channel?

ED'S FAVORITE TV SHOWS

I Love Lucy
The Donna Reed Show
Gilligan's Island
Gunsmoke
Leave It to Beaver
Our Miss Brooks
The Honeymooners
What's My Line?

---

certain measures that will make MY life better.

• Cut off cable television service and make everyone go back to Ed Anger technology—rabbit ears! That's right, folks. A good, old-fashioned antenna will pick up network TV signals the way God intended—out of the air!

• No more sign language on television. Hey, nobody supports the rights of deaf people more than yours truly. My sister is deaf in one ear and can't hear out of the other and my Uncle O.V. Potter wears a hearing aid. But former President George Bush had a great plan to end all this TV sign language years ago when he said, "Read my lips." If America had listened then, we wouldn't have all these people on television flapping their hands around like an Italian used car salesman, interfering with our God-given right to enjoy our favorite shows on the tube.

• No more worrywart warning labels spoiling our beer-drinking fun. Those same wimpy liberals who would stick warning labels on oatmeal if they could are now sticking it to a good old American institution—beer, by God! One of my all-time favorite pastimes is reading beer cans. There's a lot more interesting stuff on a brew label than on a can of pork and beans, for instance. But you stick some nincompoop warning label in

there and it ruins beer can reading for everybody. And that makes me pig-biting mad!

I drink at least a case of beer a week and have for over 30 years. And the family sawbones says I'm healthy as a horse. If beer was bad for you, then why in the hell is yours truly in such great shape? Because beer is good for you, that's why. All those docs who whined for the warning labels on beer know it, too. These rich quacks aren't stupid. If they can get more and more Americans to stop drinking good, healthy beer by scaring them to death, they'll have more patients to fleece. Let's face it, boys. About the time stories started popping up saying a few beers would stop big-bucks diseases like cancer and heart attacks, those medical money grubbers cooked up this little warning label scheme. Well, they can't fool me, by God! And they won't fool millions of American beer drinkers, either.

To commemorate the end of this warning label nonsense, and to remind us of the days when Patrick Henry and other great patriots rallied the early Americans to kick some Redcoat butt, I propose a Beer Drinkers Burp Salute every year on March 30 at 9:00 p.m., E.S.T. All of us guys down at the Dew Drop Bar and Grille will be there like clockwork, letting out one helluva collective burp. Let's hear the same from bars and taverns, bowling alleys and living room couches all across this great land of ours. It'll be The Burp Heard Round The World!

THE NATIONAL HOLIDAY PROTECTION REFORMS

Instead of blowing a whole bunch of our hard-earned tax dollars on saving spotted owls or freckled pansies or whatever, why don't we put our money where we can really do some good: preserving the sanctity of the great American holidays, like Christmas, Halloween, and the 4th of July. Here's what I've got in mind:

Boycott Artificial Christmas Trees

If God wanted us to put up fake trees for Christmas, He'd have grown them that way, by gum. Let's face it. About the only real thing left about Christmas anymore these days is a tree that smells like the great outdoors and sheds needles all over the floor.

How the hell is this boycott going to work? Easy. It's purely voluntary, but when the idiots call to invite you over for some holiday cheer, or a nice meal, just say "We'd love to come over and bring your presents, but do you have an artificial tree?" If they say yes, just hang up. Blam!

Give Your Kid a BB Gun for Christmas

What the hell is this great country coming to when a kid can't go out in the backyard and bag a few sparrows on Christmas morning, for crying out loud. I got my first Daisy Red Ryder BB

MY SUREFIRE DIET

1. If you eat something and **NOBODY SEES YOU EAT IT**, it doesn't have any calories.

2. If you drink a diet soda with a candy bar, the calories in the candy bar are canceled out by the diet soda.

3. When you eat with someone else, **CALORIES DON'T COUNT** if you don't eat more than they do.

4. Food used for medicinal purposes never counts, even hot chocolate, brandy, or cheesecake.

5. Food eaten at the movies, county fair, or the bowling alley has no calories because it's part of the **ENTIRE ENTERTAINMENT PACKAGE**—stuff like Milk Duds, buttered popcorn, Red Hots, Tootsie Rolls, and Junior Mints.

6. **FOOD LICKED OFF KNIVES AND SPOONS HAS NO CALORIES** if you are in the process of making something else—like a peanut butter sandwich or an ice cream sundae.

7. Cookie pieces have no calories at all. The process of breaking causes all the calories to leak out.

---

gun when I was just 3 years old and could pop Grandma's scrawny tomcat from 50 feet before I was 4, by gum.

So I'm calling on every patriotic parent to get up right now and go out and get your kid a BB or pellet gun for Christmas. You'll make the inventor of the first BB rifle real proud because old Abe Lincoln loved this great land of ours and he expects us to defend it, by cracky. Let's join together, friends, and make this a real Jingle Bells Shotgun Shells holiday!

Keep the Howl in Halloween

This is merely a defensive measure aimed at those wimpy bleeding hearts who are trying to ban Halloween because they claim the costumes and masks scare the bejesus out of mental patients. You heard it right, folks. A pack of shrinks are trying to outlaw my favorite holiday because a bunch of loonies have a fit when they see a monster mask or some kid dressed up like a Ninja Turtle. Wait till these knucklehead shrinks find out that when those little goblins and devils stop scaring the crap out of their patients once a year, they'll get better and won't need those big-bucks office visits anymore. I'll bet the farm when they figure that out, those docs will start running around in spider suits themselves every Halloween.

Here's the bottom line: Halloween is the one holiday that teaches America's kids not to be little scaredy-cats and jump every time somebody says "Boo!" In fact, I used to scare the daylights out of my kids every Halloween, starting way back when they were 2 years old. My boy Jimbo was scared to death of dogs when he was a toddler until I dressed up in a Doberman pinscher costume and chased him around the house. He never backed down from a dog after that—and I've seen him attack the meanest mutts in the neighborhood just to teach them a lesson.

If we don't take action to protect Halloween now, next thing you know, these nutcases will want to outlaw the full moon, for crying out loud!

The Big Old Fourth of July Smoke-In

This one's a cinch. I didn't charge up Pork Chop Hill in the Korean War so some pantywaist liberal could tell me where I can smoke and where I can't. Let's remind those anti-smoking sissies once a year that we have the right to smoke anywhere, anytime. On the Fourth of July at 4:00 p.m. Eastern Standard Time, every smoker across this great nation will simultaneously light up a smooth, satisfying smoke and slap the greasiest, smokiest meat on their barbecue grills at the same time.

The Indians sent smoke signals, didn't they? By the time the 50 million American smokers out there fire up, the squealing, pinhead anti-tobacco fanatics will think the eruption of Mount St. Helens was a Sunday School picnic. And the message we'll send will be loud and clear: Every true-blue American smoker is prepared to fight to the death, by gum, to protect their right to smoke. It's a Constitutional right. You know it. I know it. And the Supreme Court knows it.

APPLE-A-DAY HEALTH DARE ACT

You know, even President Rodham might see the wisdom in these few simple adjustments to the health care system in this country. Just call me Dr. Anger.

Free Health Care
Top of the line medical care for every real American—absolutely FREE! After we abolish all welfare, we can put those welfare folks to work in hospitals providing the free medical care I'm talking about!

The Ed Anger Medical Grade Point Average Plan

Make doctors post their medical school grades on the wall, right beside their fancy diplomas. Medical rates would vary according to the doc's grade average. For example, a doctor who maintained an A average in college would get $80 for an office visit. A sawbones with a D average would only get $20 a visit. Every doctor's office or clinic would have the average grade of its doctor or doctors painted in big block letters on a sign outside. If you are poor or broke, you could most likely get a C, D, or F doctor to see you. If you're better off, you could go to an A or B doctor for better care at a higher cost. If you needed an operation and didn't have insurance, you'd wind up under a D doctor's knife. Risky, but better than nothing.

Keep Greedy Docs Honest!

Make surgeons show us our old body parts—just like car mechanics have to when they replace a carburetor. If you're having a bad kidney cut out, for instance, they should bring it in on a tray or in a glass jar after the operation for you to see. Otherwise, they could just patch the bad one up and tell you they'd removed it. Two years later, you'd have to shell out more cash to have the same damn thing repaired. Same goes for heart transplants. You should demand that you be given your old heart to take home or flush down the toilet. That way you'd be darn sure that you'd been given a new

MY CABINET

★ **Secretary of Defense** ★
MIKE TYSON

★ **Secretary of the Treasury** ★
DONALD TRUMP

★ **Secretary of State** ★
G. GORDON LIDDY

★ **Attorney General** ★
JOHNNIE COCHRAN

★ **Secretary of Interior Decorating** ★
LIBERACE

★ **Secretary of Agriculture** ★
ROSEANNE BARR

★ **Secretary of Commerce** ★
BILL GATES

★ **Secretary of Labor** ★
LEONA HELMSLEY

★ **Secretary of Health and Human Services** ★
MARCUS WELBY, M.D.

★ **Secretary of Transportation** ★
TEDDY KENNEDY

★ **Secretary of Energy** ★
RICHARD SIMMONS

★ **Secretary of Education** ★
DIRTY HARRY

★ **Surgeon General** ★
DR. KEVORKIAN

★ **Chief Justice of the Supreme Court** ★
JUDGE WAPNER

ticker and got your money's worth. Same goes for lungs, appendixes, gallbladders, livers, cysts, assorted hysterectomy parts, and so on. Let's face it, folks. Doctors are nothing but glorified grease monkeys anyway.

And another thing. We ought to get warranties on organ transplants—just like used cars. If you have a bum lung replaced, then the transplant ought to be guaranteed for at least 90 days or 6,000 miles. I know I'm going to have what I call the American Mafia Association (AMA) raising holy hell about my new idea, but I've taken on crooks from Yale and Harvard before—when I campaigned against our Senators and Congressmen voting themselves a fat pay raise a while back.

THE CLEAN (H)AIR ACT

I've got nothing against the environment—it's just those hairy-legged potsmokers over at Greenpeace who wring their hands over a few trillion tender puffs of cigarette smoke and the so-called Greenhouse effect who get my goat. Here's what I say: Forget about the greenhouse and worry about your own house! Give the kids a bath! Trim the hedges! Order up some aluminum siding! I've got a prescription for what ails this planet:

Pop a Tire for Clean Air

According to the latest statistics, there are nearly 100 million pre-1960 cars, trucks, and buses on the planet at this very moment. So what, you say? They're all sit-

ting on at least four tires, that's what. And that's not including spares! Multiply four by 100 million and what do you get?

About 900 trillion cubic feet of good, old-fashioned air from the 1930s, 40s, and 50s, for crying out loud. My sources in the scientific community tell me that if this clean air from yesteryear was let out worldwide over a 90-day timetable, our air would be as clean as it was in 1950, maybe cleaner! We'll just give every country a day to pop all their old tires. Mexico on Monday, Germany on Tuesday, Italy on Wednesday, Canada on Thursday, New Guinea on Friday, and so on until we've popped every tire on the planet. This old stinky air we've been breathing would be forced right out of the ozone hole and disappear into space!

THE BIG STICK NATIONAL SECURITY ACT

This one's so simple I can't believe no one's ever thought of it before. Next time some two-bit country (like Haiti or Iraq) acts up on our playground, we won't wait around for the two years or more it takes the U.N. to finish deciding to tell the bad guys they're being bad. That decrepit organization can't go to the bathroom without convening a committee to study the plumbing.

Whatever happened to the good old days when we could throw our military might around all over the world in the name of

freedom and fortune? I say those days are back. The next international boil that comes to a head, we come in both barrels blazing on the very next day. No sense growing such a fine crop of soldiers if we can't take them to market! Don't think for a minute our honored Marine Corps couldn't have swept up that mess in Bosnia in about a week's time. Trust me—the world will thank us. Just like they did when the late, great General Patton almost single-handedly won World War II, putting those Nazis in their place and getting pantyhose and Hershey's chocolate into the hands of all those poor European women and children. They'll thank us, by God.

★★★★★★★★★★★★

So howza bout it?
Let's do one of those hands-across-America things—*my* America, I mean—and get this great country of ours back on its feet again. I'm asking every true-blue American voter to write in my name, Ed Anger, on the ballot so we can send a real patriot to the White House, by jiminey.

ED ANGER FOR PRESIDENT!

MADE IN U.S.A.

Send Ed Anger to the White House. Clip this button and pin it on your jacket. Cut out the bumper sticker and tape it to your car. Fill out the ballot and mail it to campaign headquarters. God Bless America!

Official Ballot
President of the United States of America

❑ **Ed Anger**

Clip and mail to: CAMPAIGN HEADQUAR-TERS, c/o Weekly World News, 600 S. East Coast Ave., Lantana, Fla. 33462

ED ANGER FOR PRESIDENT

WE OWE IT TO OURSELVES!

MY BIGGEST BEEFS
ED ANGER

EXCLUSIVE!

AND MORE...

LET'S KNOCK DOWN THE STATUE OF LIBERTY

...and tell welfare-sucking immigrants to KEEP OUT!

I'm madder than the Pilgrim who slipped off Plymouth Rock over Hillary Clinton's secret new plan to do away with America's Border Patrol.

Inside sources at the White House say she's almost convinced President Bill that trying to stop the flood of aliens into the United States costs too much—and that all that money should be poured into her National Health Care scheme.

"Hillary has really put her foot down on this one," said one senior administration aide.

"She wants to give every foreigner free entry into America.

"If Haiti's entire population ends up in Florida, that would be hunky-dory with her.

"She wants to take the taxpayer money we're now spending to keep aliens out of the country and use it to pay for free medical treatment for sick illegals. Maybe this makes sense to

Hillary, but I don't get it."

And what makes me really pig-biting mad is the latest Carnegie-Atex study on population shifts in America. Here, my friends, is a little statistic that ought to set off alarm bells from sea to shining sea.

The study found that immigrants will outnumber real Americans by nearly 3 to 1 in just ten years!

And English will be the third most popular language in this country—right behind Spanish and that Creole gibberish the Haitians speak, for crying out loud.

Let's face it, folks. If we don't do something about this tidal wave of immigrants who are

The Statue of Liberty has been welcoming foreigners to America for more than 100 years—and Ed is sick and tired of it!

bleeding Uncle Sam dry, it's our own fault.

And I think we ought to start by kicking over the Statue of Liberty, by jiminey.

Hey, the statue was great when we needed all those tired and hungry masses to do those no-brainer jobs that nobody else wanted. But hell, now we've got college grads to fill those jobs, by gum.

In other words, we've got enough homegrown good-for-nothings without having to import 'em from Mexico or Haiti.

But anyway, back to pulling

down the Statue of Liberty. If you don't think THAT would send a signal that we mean business about stopping immigration, you're crazy.

So just start humming the "Battle Hymn of the Republic" right now and join the rest of us patriotic Americans in standing up for the old Red, White, and Blue.

Just fill out this STATUE OF LIBERTY POLL.

If you don't, we may soon be eatin' tacos and bananas instead of hot dogs and hamburgers at our Fourth of July picnics.

Ed Anger

ED ANGER'S
STATUE OF LIBERTY POLL

☐ **YES:** I agree with Ed Anger that we ought to have tug-boats pull the Statue of Liberty into New York Harbor as soon as possible. Immigrants are feeding on America like flies on a birthday cake.

☐ **NO:** Even if immigrants are breeding like rabbits and bleeding America dry, we shouldn't pull the Statue of Liberty down. Let's give it back to France, instead.

Mail your vote to: STATUE OF LIBERTY POLL, Weekly World News, 600 S. East Coast Ave., Lantana, Fla. 33462

FRY DEATH ROW CREEPS IN
ELECTRIC BLEACHERS!

I'm madder than a tomcat with his tail in a light socket over this latest bleeding-heart campaign to outlaw capital punishment.

If our Founding Fathers didn't believe we should fry killers and rapists like pieces of bacon, they wouldn't have mentioned the electric chair in the Declaration of Independence, for crying out loud!

But if the whining, sniveling liberals want to stop these weekly executions of human cockroaches, then I've got a wonderful solution.

Let's kill 'em all once a year in electric bleachers!

You heard me right, folks. We could hot-wire portable bleachers like you see at Little League baseball games and zap up to 500 sex fiends, murderers, and crooked congressmen at the same time. Just file 'em into these cheap

...and get rid of 'em all at once!

seats at gunpoint, tell 'em to have a seat, and hit the juice.

The thing would light up like a backyard bug zapper, by gum. It'll sound like about 10,000 hamburger patties sizzling on the grill!

And let's face it. The prissy, squealing liberals would only have to scream about capital punishment once a year instead of every damn day!

Legend has it that our late, great President Abe Lincoln ordered the first double electrocution in a crudely wired porch swing.

The device was effective if not efficient—it took nearly six hours on high before the two men accused of raping a young schoolmarm finally died.

"The meat just fell off the bones when they were pulled out of the electric swing," said one eyewitness in a diary discovered some 20 years after the execution in 1883.

Our best Death Row statistics say there are over 800 of these human scum currently awaiting their one-way trip to Hell—if you get my drift. And their room and board is costing hardworking American taxpayers nearly 34.7 million dollars a year! So my electric bleachers idea is sounding better all the time—right, folks?

Ed Anger

IT AIN'T CHRISTMAS WITHOUT THE GIFT OF GUNS!

I'm madder than Santa Claus stuck in the chimney over my thunderthighs daughter-in-law, Candy, pitching a hissy fit when I bought my grandson a shotgun for Christmas!

Just because he's only five years old doesn't mean he's too young to start putting some meat on the table. My dad gave me my first gun when I was just three and let me shoot a chicken every time we wanted one for supper, by jiminey!

Dad even let me bag our old milk cow when she got too old to produce anymore.

I took her down at 20 yards with one shot from my trusty .22—when I was just six, for crying out loud.

Let's face it. If these whiney, sniveling women's libbers and animal lovers get their way, guns will be outlawed and we'll have a whole generation of homosexuals on our hands.

Everybody knows sissy boys don't like playing with guns and ammo.

So they usually grow up to be prancing little fairies who powder their noses and wear lipstick. And if my lardbutt daughter-in-law had anything to say about it, my grandson, Teddy, would probably grow up listening to Liberace instead of pumping hot lead into living things with yours truly.

Every young man in America ought to have a handgun AND a rifle—and know how to use them, for Christmas' sake!

If our Founding Fathers hadn't let their little boys learn to shoot rabbits, squirrels, beavers, and birds, how the hell would they have known how to shoot Indians when they grew up?

Then where would we be, huh? Sitting around Christmas dinner in a tepee, that's where!

I'm going to take little Teddy out in the backyard and let him shoot anything he wants within reason—my old dog Dodger excluded, of course.

But if his mother's stupid cat pokes his head out of the bushes, I'm going to let Teddy open up on that critter with both barrels—and have his first kill stuffed and mounted!

I want to wish all our *Weekly World News* readers out there a Merry Christmas and Happy New Year.

It's the great Americans like you who give me the courage to tell it like it is in my columns all year long.

If our Founding Fathers hadn't let their little boys learn to shoot rabbits, squirrels, beavers, and birds, how the hell would they have known how to shoot Indians when they grew up?

LET'S ABOLISH SOCIAL SECURITY!

I'm madder than Hillary Clinton with an empty tube of cellulite cream over all this hand-wringing about Social Security, Medicare, Medicaid, and all those other bleeding-heart liberal government handouts.

Let's just balance the gol-durned budget, for crying out loud, and quit whining about it. I say we abolish EVERY federal charity program on New Year's Day. And to put my money where my mouth is, I'm turning in my Social Security card first thing in the morning.

Let's face it. I love guns and keep 'em all over the house—fully loaded, by gum. But I've gotta hand it to President Bush for ripping up his National Rifle Association membership in the wake of the Oklahoma City bombing. A man's gotta do what a man's gotta do. And now, my fellow Americans, I'm taking the same kind of stand so we can get this great nation back on sound financial footing: I'll not cash another of my Social Security checks until the day I die.

My poor old granddaddy, God bless his soul, got by on what he saved for his golden years—and didn't need some Socialist giveaway to do it. And when he and my grandmother got sick, they didn't bother going to a doctor or hospital unless they had the cash to pay for their treatment, by golly.

Isn't it about time that Americans went back to pulling on their bootstraps to get by rather than sitting by the mailbox waiting for another Social Security or Medicare check to arrive?

But what makes me so pig-biting mad is all this blubbering, weepy-eyed liberal crap about how we can't let people go without welfare or medical care. I say, why the hell not? Americans went without government charity from 1776 until 1940 when that pinko Franklin Roosevelt dreamed up Social Security to get reelected.

The only thing Social Security has done is make older Americans fat, soft, and lazy. Most of 'em ought to be working

We can balance the budget INSTANTLY with this bold new plan...

for a living rather than playing golf or cluttering up the countryside in their stupid motor homes. So I'm all for raising the legal retirement age to 95. If that doesn't solve the stupid Social Security crisis, I'll eat my hat. By the time anybody became eligible for benefits, they'd be strapped in a chair gumming baby food and waiting to kick off, by golly.

And as for all this free medical care everybody's come to depend on—I say let's end it all right now. Real Americans don't take charity—and that's telling it like it is.

Ed Anger

ED ANGER SOCIAL SECURITY POLL

☐ **YES:** I agree with Ed Anger that Social Security should be abolished on New Year's Day, and that older Americans ought to get off their butts and get back to work.

☐ **NO:** Without Social Security, Medicare, and the like, millions of Americans would go down the tubes. Ed's idea is lunacy and I'll fight it every step of the way.

Clip and mail to: **ED ANGER SOCIAL SECURITY POLL,** c/o Weekly World News, 600 S. East Coast Ave., Lantana, Fla. 33462

LETTERS TO ED

Thousands of *Weekly World News* readers can't be wrong: Ed Anger is a fool for suggesting that we can balance the federal budget by abolishing Social Security. A staggering 99.7% of the 62,032 readers that responded to the column disagreed with Ed, most of them angrily:

"I paid Social Security taxes for over 50 years, and now that I'm handicapped and unable to work, I need my Social Security checks just to exist. If Ed Anger wants to send his checks back to the government, that's his right. Just don't mess with the little bit of money I need to survive."

—J.P., Pensacola, FL

"Social Security is for rich old geezers who want to live a life of luxury on the backs of young adults like me. I say banish Social Security as soon as possible—before the whole damn country goes bankrupt."

—D.J., Boston, MA

GET RID OF MEDICARE, TOO, FOR CRYING OUT LOUD!

COMPUTER NERDS MAKE ME SICK!

I'm madder than a computer nerd with a busted mouse that the editor of *The Weekly World News* has put America's greatest tabloid on America Online.

I didn't charge up Pork Chop Hill in Korea back in May of '52 with my machine gun blazing to end up sitting in front of some stupid computer screen educating a bunch of social misfits on what it takes to be a REAL American.

But, hey, let's face it. As long as I get a fat paycheck every week, I'd preach to a bunch of lisping, limp-wristed, flag-burning pansies, for crying out loud. So what's so different about a gang of pencil-necked geeks who hang out on America Online because nobody else will talk to them—and especially the babes.

But what makes me so pig-biting mad about this idiotic American Online stuff is that I can't write any columns about sports. Everybody knows that computer nerds throw baseballs like girls and think a football is something you sit on while playing chess or some other sissy game.

These guys wouldn't know the World Wrestling Federation from the New York City Ballet, for Pete's sake. I'm getting so hot under the collar just thinking about it, I'll probably have to take another shot of Old Crow just to calm down.

And another thing! Some bubbleheaded lady reporter who works here in the office just told me there are 3 million of these computer wackos tapped into America Online and their numbers are swelling by the second.

I think that's great. At least it keeps these nerds from hanging around Office Depot, picking their noses. In fact, Raymond Thill Sr., the only real nerd that I know personally, spends days at a time lurking around computer stores—even though, like most cybernuts, old Ray's too cheap to ever buy anything.

Hey, I wasn't born yesterday. I know there are some girls yakking away on America Online. But I'll guarantee you that every one of them is fat and ugly.

If they weren't, they'd be strutting their stuff poolside in one of those thong bikinis instead of plopping down in front of their computer with a box of bonbons.

I'll be blunt with you. You wouldn't want to go for the last pork chop on the platter if one of these America Online gals had her eye on it. You'd probably get a fork through the back of your hand, by jiminey.

Bottom line time, folks. Men who like computers are skinny, effeminate wusses. The myth is that all of them wear thick glasses, but that's just a myth. The latest Carnegie-Atex Poll says only 87 percent of them wear pop-bottle specs.

And women who dig computers are porkers, plain and simple.

And if you can't handle the truth, you can byte my butt, buckaroos.

...and cyber chicks are FAT AND UGLY!!!

MARTHA STEWART IS THE <u>PERFECT</u> ROLE MODEL FOR AMERICAN WOMEN!

I'm madder than a feminist with a busted Harley over all the flak that top TV housewife Martha Stewart is taking over her great new show.

Those yappy women's libbers and female politicians are squealing bloody murder because Martha Stewart preaches that women ought to do the things they are good at—things like cooking, sewing, crafts, laundry, and washing dishes.

And most women who don't have their bras hooked too tight will agree with me.

Let's face it. The dog-eat-dog world that men work in every day is no place for a woman and it never has been, for crying out loud.

If we needed women to work, then why in hell did they stay at home for 200 years while men built this great nation from the ground up?

Oh sure. A few heavyweight gals shot rivets into airplanes back in WWII. But those gals could swing a 12-lb. hammer like John Henry, if you get my drift.

But the real reason I think that this "Martha Stewart Living" TV show ought to be required viewing is that it teaches little girls what they REALLY should be when they grow up.

America needs devoted, highly-skilled housewives now more than ever.

And if we don't get our ladies back in the house where they belong, who is going to operate the high-tech dishwashers, Dustbusters and microwaves us men will be inventing in the future?

I mean, these things aren't the easiest things to turn on if you don't know what you're doing.

But most importantly, women are happier when they stay at home and putter around the house—and Martha Stewart has the smile to prove it. You don't see her trotting off to work every day, by jiminey!

She looks more contented than the Carnation cow, if you're old enough to remember those ads. Besides, if God had meant for women to hold full-time jobs, He'd have made 'em stronger or smarter.

Martha Stewart might not be a rocket scientist, but she's pretty as a picture and handy around the house—where it counts!

MARTHA POLL

☐ **YES:** I agree with Ed that American women ought to be more like the perfect housewife Martha Stewart.

☐ **NO:** I think Ed Anger is an idiot. Millions of American women have to work AND keep house because their bum husbands won't do either.

Clip and mail to: ED ANGER MARTHA STEWART POLL, c/o Weekly World News, 600 S. East Coast Ave., Lantana, Fla. 33462

CRIMINALS LIVING IN LUXURY APARTMENTS!

This is an OUTRAGE, fellow Americans!

I'm madder than the Birdman of Alcatraz with a dead parakeet over the latest liberal crusade to make life more comfy for the inmates in our country's prisons.

Believe it or not, Congress is seriously considering a lunatic plan to get rid of jail cells and give murderers, rapists, and child molesters their own plush apartments to lounge around in at tax-payers' expense.

Each prisoner would have his own little home, complete with a bedroom, a kitchen equipped with all the modern appliances, a study complete with a home computer, a private bathroom, nice big windows, and a goldurned lawn, for crying out loud!

No, my friends, I'm not kidding.

What most of us working stiffs bust our tails to own, criminals would get for free just by raping or killing somebody. Is this sick or what?

Instead of being cooped up in cell blocks like the animals they are, each con would live in the lap of luxury, get to fix his own food, tend his own garden, and spend his spare time reading or playing computer games.

The bleeding-heart nitwits who support this crazy scheme say it would teach inmates to be pro-ductive, responsible members of society.

And I say that's bull dookey.

What we're really talking about here, folks, is a quiet, tree-lined subdivision for criminals. The only difference between these new prisons and any other subur-ban neighborhood would be the barbed wire fences.

But of course it's not going to be long before they have to put a barbed wire fence around my development because they just built a public school down the street. And Sing Sing ain't got nothing on public schools when

it comes to housing criminals.

But what makes me so pig-bit-ing mad is that patriotic Amer-icans won't have a thing to say about this prison insanity after liberal Clinton Democrats in Congress hop on the bandwagon and give it the go-ahead. The only prayer we've got against this nonsense is if every real Amer-ican stands up and screams at the top of his lungs, "I'm pig-biting mad, and I'm not going to take it anymore!"

President Hillary and her hus-band Bill might think they can force this prison reform crap down our ignorant throats, but this time they're dead wrong, by gum.

"Most Americans just don't realize what tough childhoods these criminals had," Hillary whined at a recent talk before the Committee for Fair Treatment of Parolees. "We're going to give

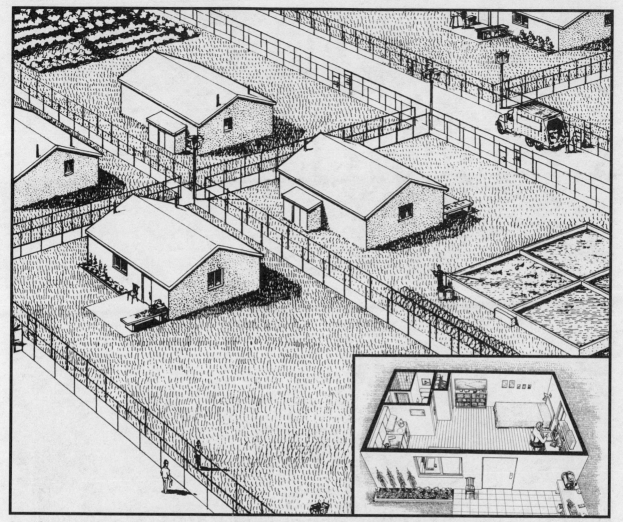

Murderers, rapists, and child molesters would live in cozy prison neighborhoods like this one.

them a chance to prove they can be productive, responsible citizens with a little help from us. Let's all show some compassion and get the apartment prison program on track as rapidly as possible, regardless of the cost."

If you had told me ten years ago that those words would come from an American president, I would have moved to Costa Rica right then, for crying out loud.

The next thing you and I know, Hillary will say that we should build one of these plush apartments for every illegal immigrant who sneaks into this great nation.

Well, this is the last straw. If the Clintons are re-elected to the White House in 1996, the whole Anger family is getting the hell out of this country and going someplace where real Americans have a fighting chance—like Mexico, maybe. And would the last real American across the border please bring the flag?

INDIANS WANT TO SCALP THE WASHINGTON REDSKINS!

ED'S ON THE WARPATH TO SAVE AN AMERICAN INSTITUTION!

I'm madder than General Custer at the Little Big Horn over this latest attack on the Washington Redskins pro-football team.

Senator Ben Nighthorse Campbell, a Scottish Indian, is leading the fight to make the Redskins change their name to the Washington Native Americans or some such crap.

The Colorado Democrat sniffs that "The name Redskins is offensive to Indian people. Whether it is considered offensive by non-Indians is not the issue."

Well, excuuuuuuuuuse me, Chief!

What is this great country coming to when you can't name sports teams after colorful minorities like Indians, for crying out loud?

And talk about offensive, what about the name "Nighthorse"? If I lived on the reservation, I'd be hopping mad over these liberal politicians giving themselves names like Nighthorse or Mud-In-The-Face or Bee-Up-The-Butt or any of those old tribal names.

Not that I care that much about the stupid Washington Redskins. I'm a Dallas Cowboys fan, myself. Always go with a winner, I always say.

But I'll be damned if I'll stand by while some yahoo redskin like Senator Campbell tries to change the name of an American institution just so he can get some votes.

Let's face it, folks. You wouldn't hear a peep out of anybody if the team was called the Washington Whiteskins, now would you?

What kind of firewater are you drinking, Senator Campbell? Why don't you stick to playing your tom-tom!

And what will they want to change the names of next? Great children's books like "The Little Injun That Could"?

And another thing: Where did the name Campbell come from, Senator? Huh? Huh?

The tribes that live in the Highlands of Scotland, that's where, you forked tongue phony.

All you're looking for is another feather in your headdress with this ambush on the Redskins football team.

Jim Thorpe, that great Indian football player, must be doing push-ups in his grave over all this nonsense. It was Thorpe, you might recall, who headed the battle to get the Washington team called the Redskins in the first place.

Indians gave us ticket scalpers but they also gave us the great games of basketball and bingo. America should honor this great heritage by naming more teams Redskins or Renegades or Screaming Squaws, by gum.

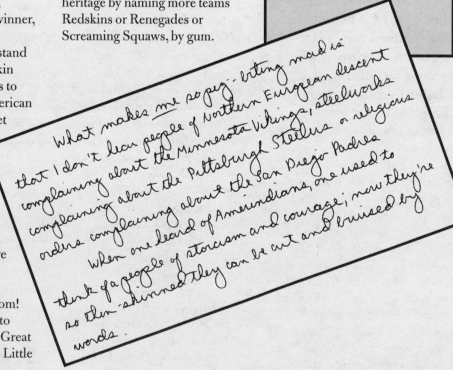

What makes me so peg-biting mad is that I don't hear people of Northern European descent complaining about the Minnesota Vikings, or steelworkers complaining about the Pittsburgh Steelers or religious orders complaining about the San Diego Padres. When one heard of Amerindians, one used to think of a people of stoicism and courage; now they're so thin-skinned they can be cut and bruised by words.

FANCY-PANTS FRENCH RESTAURANTS ARE A BIG

I'm madder than a bullfrog with a charley horse over what happened to me the other night at one of those fancy-schmancy restaurants that rich people go to.

For our 39th wedding anniversary, Thelma Jean hoodwinked me into taking her to our town's only French restaurant—Le Chalet Renoir or something like that.

A quiet little booth at the Sizzler steakhouse would have suited me just fine, but Noooooooo! She has to go someplace where everything on the damned menu is "Chef's Surprise" because you can't read a word of it. I mean, they could have All-U-Can-Eat Shrimp on the menu and you'd never know it!

The waitress at the Chinese takeout doesn't bat an eye when I order No. 5 on their menu, but when I tried it with this snooty French waiter, he asked if that was a bottle of wine. I said, "Hell, no, it's the No. 5 dinner, you idiot!"

I ordered the same thing for Thelma Jean so she wouldn't be embarrassed trying to order something she couldn't read.

The swishy waiter finally brought out a couple of plates of white sauce with a little lump of meat in the middle and two green beans the chef forgot to cook.

Not bad for an appetizer, whatever it was, I thought. Thelma Jean lapped it up like a hog in a chocolate factory. And then we waited for the main course.

For a gol-durned hour we sat there listening to some twinkle-toes play French songs on the piano. And I got pig-biting mad, too, when I asked him to play "Frere Jacques" and he looked at me like I was from Planet X.

After another half hour, I snapped my fingers at our fairy waiter—and the nincompoop brought me the bill, for Pete's sake!

I thought the only place you got the bill BEFORE dinner was Burger King.

"Where the hell is our dinner?" I asked. Then the pinhead tells me we ate it over an hour ago. Thelma Jean burst into tears and ran out of the place.

If rich people are so damn smart, why do they eat at restaurants where the more you pay, the less food you get?

On the way home, we swung by Kentucky Fried Chicken for a real meal—spicy wings, mashed potatoes, and two large root beers!

Ed Anger

PAVE THE STUPID RAINFORESTS!

I'm madder than a monkey with a rotten banana over all this hullabaloo about saving the stupid rainforests in South America.

Wimpy environmentalists are crying big fat tears because a bunch of head-hunters in Brazil are chopping down some trees to make a little extra spending money.

Jungles would look better this way, says Ed.

These fruitcake Chicken Littles believe if we chop up jungles there won't be any more air and we'll all die.

Hogwash! They can PAVE the darn rainforests for all I care.

Let's face it. The first thing our Founding Fathers did when they landed on America's shores was start cutting down trees.

George Washington and Thomas Jefferson were farsighted enough to know that you can't build shopping malls in the woods, for crying out loud.

Our great nation doesn't have one single rainforest and I'm breathing just fine, thank you.

If the rainforests are so healthy, then why in hell are all the people who live there trying to come here?

And another thing. The nuclear plant protesters who scream doom and gloom about the rainforests are the same nutcases who believe in this ozone stuff.

You know, there's supposed to be a hole in the ozone layer over the North Pole or something and we're all supposed to get cancer and die because it lets too much sunshine in. Phooey!

It's supposed to be caused by all those cans of spray paint we've used to make America more beautiful. So let's just put ozone in spray cans and sell it to these scaredy-cat environmentalists.

These yellow bellies could just spray it into the air and patch the hole over the North Pole in no time flat.

I mean, how difficult can it be to put ozone in a can?

And while I'm on the subject, I'll tell you another thing. These bleeding-heart nature freaks say they want to save the rainforests and all that stuff for our children. That's a crock.

Ask any red-blooded American teenager where he'd rather be—in a nice air-conditioned shopping mall playing video games or slapping mosquitoes in some godforsaken jungle?

GIVE TEACHERS STUN GUNS

TO CONTROL BAD KIDS!

I'm happier than a second-grader with a shiny new switchblade that Congress is finally considering one of my greatest ideas ever—to let school teachers zap unruly brats with stun guns!

That's right folks...stun guns. Let's face it. You're safer in downtown Bosnia these days than you are in Geography 101.

And I for one think that our great teachers have been bullied by seven-year-old criminals long enough, by gum.

Back in 1991, yours truly suggested that teachers be allowed to keep the little hoodlums in line with high-voltage guns that would give them a jolt to remember the minute they started stirring up trouble.

And now, my sources tell me that Congress will take up the Anger proposal the minute they get this budget nonsense out of the way.

And I say it's about time, by jiminy.

Give those little creeps about 20,000 volts between the eyes and you'll see them straighten up pronto.

Not enough to kill 'em, you understand, but enough to make 'em think twice before they toss that next spitball.

All those late, great teachers like TV's "Our Miss Brooks" never had to pack a pistol to keep order in the classroom in the 1950s. She'd just purse her lips and stare the little devils down.

But try staring down one of today's ten-year-old school yard thugs and you'll get a baseball bat upside the head.

And another thing. Half the punks in public school today are there because we refuse to send the little criminals to the peniten-

Just **ZAP** the crap out of these Future Murderers of America when they're five!

If teachers were armed with stun guns they wouldn't have much trouble keeping the kids in line, Ed says.

tiary where they belong.

Just zap the crap out of these Future Murderers of America when they're 5 and we won't have to fry 'em in the electric chair when they're 20, for Pete's sake.

If our teachers shock the day-

lights out of these monsters every time they screw up, maybe normal children can go back to the

Ed Anger

COPYCAT RUSSKIES STOLE *OLD GLORY!*

I'm madder than Uncle Sam with bubble gum in his beard over the new Russian flag—'cause the damned thing's red, white, and blue, for crying out loud!

Let's face it. I'm as happy as the next guy that those slimy commies and their hammer and sickle flag are history, but some things are just too much to swallow.

And this copycat flag is one of 'em. Betsy Ross, who sewed the first Old Glory back in 1775, must be banging her head against the lid of her star-spangled coffin.

I almost blew a gasket when these new Russian capitalists put a McDonald's in the middle of Moscow.

But the metal plate in my head is hotter than a firecracker over this Russkie flag business.

How long before they add a few stars to the darn thing? And some stripes can't be far behind, now can they?

If the Russians want to be like America so much, why don't they apply for statehood like Hawaii and Alaska did?

Then they could fly the real thing instead of coming up with a clearly inferior red, white, and blue design of their own.

Or maybe we could sell 'em the copyright to Old Glory and make a few bucks to cut the budget

BEWARE: Next they'll be humming the Star-Spangled Banner, by gum!

36

deficit, by jiminy. But what makes me so pig-biting mad is that my sources in Moscow tell me that Boris Yeltsin is considering stealing our National Anthem!

You heard it right, folks. Big Boris has an old 45 record of that late, great 1950s singer Kate Smith singing "The Anthem" on the flip side of "God Bless America." And he plays it constantly, according to his closest pals. But unless Boris wants to be on the target end of our nukes again, he'd better think twice about even humming our national tune.

And if he wants to put some stuff on his red, white, and blue flag, fine—as long as there's a Wal-Mart built in Russia for every star or stripe they put on it!

Ed Anger

DO YOU AGREE WITH ED?
ED ANGER FLAG POLL

☐ **YES:** I agree with Ed Anger that the Russians have no right to use red, white, and blue on their flag and if they don't change it—nuke 'em!

☐ **NO:** The Russians have every right to steal our red, white, and blue for their flag and Ed Anger is an idiot for objecting to it.

Clip and mail to: **ED ANGER'S FLAG POLL,**
c/o Weekly World News,
600 S. East Coast Avenue, Lantana, Fla. 33462

Ed Anger,

What an idiot you are! I'm Ed-biting mad that you're accusing the Russians of stealing our national colors. Don't you see they're trying to join our team? Those stupid Ruskies feel like the last kid on the playground to get picked to play kickball. They're scared of being left all alone in Siberia without anyone to bring 'em vodka and quiche. Now I'm not saying we let 'em join our team. You won't find me playing badminton with Boris or air hockey with Anatoly, but at least we know who's kissing whose butt. And it's a lot easier to keep an eye on those sneaky bastards that way.

U.S. GOVERNMENT TO BLAME FOR LETTING BAT BOY ESCAPE!

I'm madder than Batman with a run in his tights over a recent front page story in *Weekly World News***.**

Just how in the hell do you let something as dangerous as this "bat boy" escape from a high security research facility? I'll tell you how—the U.S. government must be running it.

Our late, great President Harry S. Truman must be twirling in his grave at the bumbling idiots our once-proud security forces have become.

The CIA, FBI, and Secret Service aren't worth a hill of beans between them anymore.

Once those commie cockroaches got stomped on in Russia, our national defense forces went straight to hell, folks.

Nothing to worry about anymore, right?

Big-time wrong, my friends.

Now we've got this "bat boy" on the loose and the bleeding-heart liberals are already coming out of the woodwork.

"We mustn't forget that this child evolved as a cave dweller and knows nothing about our

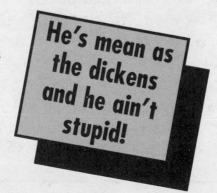

He's mean as the dickens and he ain't stupid!

society and civilization.

"I hope and pray that we are able to capture him before anybody gets hurt," sniffed Dr. Ron Dillon.

This Dillon dingbat was the egghead in charge of studying this little devil when he escaped near Wheeling, West Virginia.

What Dr. Dillon doesn't tell you is that this two-foot tall demon has teeth like Gillette razor blades and a tongue like a Brillo pad.

He's got eyes the size of Ping-Pong balls that let him find you in the dark and a set of ears as big as a small catcher's mitt. That's so he can hear his prey running up to a mile away.

My sources in the Pentagon tell me the danger is REAL, folks.

Now Dr. Dillon would have us believe that this creature, found deep in a West Virginia cave last May, eats about 20 lbs. of insects a day. Baloney! Look at this kid. If he runs out of bugs, miniature poodles start to look awfully tasty.

Be on the lookout for a half-human bat boy that escaped from a West Virginia research facility.

What's next on the little fiend's menu—humans? You betcha!

The scientists who were studying this "bat boy" when he made a run for it swear he isn't one IQ point smarter than a chimp.

Believe that and I've got a bridge to sell you. You can look at this thing and tell he's no dummy.

And if he's so stupid, why have authorities from coast to coast and particularly in West Virginia, Virginia, Kentucky, Tennessee, North Carolina, Ohio, and Pennsylvania been warned to be on the lookout for the thing?

I'll tell you why—he's mean as the dickens and he ain't stupid. He may be the biggest threat to the U.S. since Hurricane Andrew. I'm going to keep my eyes peeled for this bat brat.

I suggest you do the same.

TODAY'S COUNTRY MUSIC STARS ARE A BUNCH OF CITY SLICKERS!

I'm madder than Hank Williams with a smashed cowboy hat over this latest crop of so-called country music singers.

My bubbleheaded daughter-in-law, Candy—who's so fat she has to put a bookmark in a neck wrinkle to find her pearls—is a big Garth Brooks fan, for instance.

Garth Brooks, folks, is about as country as John Travolta. This guy never even saw a horse until he was 20 years old, for crying out loud. And even then he thought it was a cow. The closest he's ever been to a farm is the vegetable section at the supermarket!

Old Hank must be trying to claw out of his grave after listening to these city slickers making a farce out of the music that made America great.

The hottest "country" star going is this Billy Ray Cyrus who Candy drools over like a hunk of fudge. This guy would sit backwards on a tractor, for Pete's sake. He's got a punk rock hairdo and throws his leg up in the air like Herman and the Hermits. And not only that, he wears tennis shoes on stage.

I was country when country wasn't cool and I know a real country singer when I hear one—guys like Porter Wagoner, Merle Haggard, Randy Travis, Loretta Lynn, and my personal favorite, George Jones.

I was watching "The Grand Ole Opry" on TV the other day when some gal named Mary Chapin Carpenter did a number. First off, no real country gal would use two last names. And not only that, she went to some fancy-pants girls' college called Vassar. Anybody knows no real country singer ever bothered to finish high school, by cracky.

You really think this gal has ever plunked her butt down in an outhouse—or has ever even seen one for that matter?

And another thing. These new "country" stars don't even drink—and they're damn proud of it. Now just how in hell are you going to be a real country singer without drinkin' whiskey and gettin' drunk? Let's face it. That's what country music is all about.

I've got a good-ole-boy buddy named Joe Berger who's about to become the hottest new country songwriter in Nashville. Joe's so country he eats catfish and hog brains for breakfast. "These new country singers are so citified that a plate of collards would kill 'em dead," says Joe.

And if Garth, Billy Ray, and Mary Chapin don't get back on the rock 'n roll tour where they belong—"The Grand Ole Opry" will be sounding just like "American Bandstand."

Ed Anger

JOE BERGER IS SO COUNTRY HE EATS CATFISH AND HOG BRAINS ... FOR BREAKFAST!

LETTERS TO ED

Yes, I agree with Ed that this new crop of citified country singers like Garth Brooks & Billy Ray Cyrus ought to be banned from the grand ole opry.

—LD, Oklahoma City, OK

The first time Ronnie Millsap walked out on the Grand Ol Opry Stage and ran his fingers down the keyborad I knew then that country as this country knows it was "Finished." I can fully understand why all the "Boys" left Nashville for Silver Dollar City, MO.

—SA, Little Rock, AK

Why don't you try to get on stage and sing. I don't think there is anything wrong with our country singers today. I have seen your personal favorite, George Jones, and he is a beached whale and seal mixed together. You listen to me pinhead. These singers don't need trash like you shooting them down.

—JB, Sault Ste Marie, ON

Grand Ole Opry superstar Garth Brooks "is about as country as John Travolta," says Ed Anger.

DO YOU AGREE WITH ED?

ED ANGER COUNTRY MUSIC POLL

☐ **YES:** I agree with Ed that this new crop of citified country singers like Garth Brooks and Billy Ray Cyrus ought to be banned from "The Grand Ole Opry."

☐ **NO:** It's about time country music started sounding like rap or rock 'n roll instead of hick tunes from the sticks.

Send your response to:
ED ANGER'S COUNTRY MUSIC POLL, Weekly World News, 600 S. East Coast Ave., Lantana, Fla. 33462

BAN THIS <u>STUPID DOGGIE</u> I.Q. LIST!

I'm so pig-biting mad this week I could suck the scales off a live rattlesnake!

Some airhead psychology professor just ranked the intelligence of 132 breeds of dogs—and the kook put English bull terriers like my dog Dodger 118th on his list.

Prof. Stanley Coren is peddling a book called *The Intelligence of Dogs*, and if you ask me, it ought to be banned in every state in the union.

Why? Because it's full of lies, that's why. Nobody should be allowed to spread this poison. Let's face it. I can put up with somebody calling my daughter-in-law, Candy, stupid. I can even put up with somebody saying my wife, Thelma Jean, isn't playing with a full deck. And I'll be the first to admit that my kids were "slow learners."

But nobody, and I mean nobody, calls my dog dumb. I'd shoot somebody for less. In fact, I'm so upset, I'm going to have to take another shot of Old Crow and two aspirin just to calm down enough to finish writing

FETCH YOUR OWN DAMN BALL!

this column.

What this nincompoop "dog expert" did to get his idiotic canine I.Q. list was to ask a bunch of pansy dog show judges which dogs were the most obedient, for crying out loud—NOT which dogs were the smartest.

Now you tell me, which dog is smarter—some dumb-butt border collie (rated No. 1) who'll run and jump in a lake on command or my dog Dodger (No. 118) who'll just sit there and tell YOU to go jump in a lake? And another thing. My dog Dodger won't sit, stay, roll over, play dead, or do any of those other stupid dog tricks. So what? He barks at the EXACT time his favorite TV show, "Wheel of Fortune," comes on—and he even whines during the commercials.

He uses the toilet and flushes it himself when it's too cold or rainy to go outside. And he can pop a top on a beer without spilling a drop—something he just started doing out of the blue when he was seven months old.

Dodger won't even ride in the car unless you fasten a seat belt around him first. Where the hell he learned that, I'll never know. Probably from television.

This poodle-brained professor finally 'fesses up and admits his ratings focus on obedience I.Q. and not instinctive intelligence or the ability to solve problems. Which is exactly what my dog Dodger is great at—problem solving and instinctive intelligence.

The more tricks a dog will do, the stupider he is, I say. If Dodger wanted to fetch and heel and all that dog show crap, he could do it in a minute. He just doesn't want to.

And besides being smarter than any dog in that nutty professor's top ten, he can kick the bejesus out of those other mutts any day of the week. Count on it.

Ed Anger

How Does YOUR Dog Rate?

After consulting dog obedience judges in the U.S. and Canada, Stanley Coren, author of *The Intelligence of Dogs*, ranked 132 pedigreed pooches according to their ability to learn owner-pleasing behavior.

1. Border collie
2. Poodle
3. German shepherd
4. Golden retriever
5. Doberman pinscher
6. Shetland sheepdog
7. Labrador retriever
8. Papillon
9. Rottweiler
10. Australian cattle dog
11. Pembroke Welsh corgi
12. Miniature schnauzer
13. English springer spaniel
14. Belgian Tervuren
15. Schipperke
(tie) Belgian sheepdog
17. Collie
(tie) Keeshond
19. German shorthaired pointer
20. Flat-coated retriever
(tie) English cocker spaniel
(tie) Standard schnauzer
23. Brittany spaniel
24. Cocker spaniel
25. Weimaraner
26. Belgian Malinois
27. Bernese mountain dog
28. Pomeranian
29. Irish water spaniel
30. Vizsla
31. Cardigan Welsh corgi
32. Chesapeake Bay retriever
33. Puli
(tie) Yorkshire terrier
35. Giant schnauzer
(tie) Portuguese water dog
37. Airedale
(tie) Bouvier des Flandres
39. Border terrier
40. Welsh springer spaniel
41. Manchester terrier
42. Samoyed
43. Field spaniel
(tie) Newfoundland
(tie) Australian terrier
(tie) Am. Staffordshire terrier
(tie) Gordon setter
(tie) Bearded collie

49. Cairn terrier
(tie) Kerry blue terrier
(tie) Irish setter
52. Norwegian elkhound
53. Affenpinscher
(tie) Silky terrier
(tie) Miniature pinscher
(tie) English setter
(tie) Pharaoh hound
(tie) Clumber spaniel
59. Norwich terrier
60. Dalmatian
61. Soft-coated wheaten terrier
(tie) Bedlington terrier
(tie) Smooth-haired fox terrier
64. Curly-coated retriever
(tie) Irish wolfhound
66. Kuvasz
(tie) Australian shepherd
68. Saluki
(tie) Finnish spitz
(tie) Pointer
71. Cavalier King Charles spaniel
(tie) German wirehaired spaniel
(tie) Black and tan coonhound
(tie) American water spaniel
75. Siberian husky
(tie) Bichon frise
(tie) English toy spaniel
78. Tibetan spaniel
(tie) English foxhound
(tie) Otter hound
(tie) American foxhound
(tie) Greyhound
(tie) Wirehaired pointing griffon
84. West Highland white terrier
(tie) Scottish deerhound
86. Boxer
(tie) Great Dane
88. Dachshund
(tie) Stafford bull terrier
90. Alaskan malamute
91. Whippet
(tie) Chinese shar-pei

(tie) Wirehaired fox terrier
94. Rhodesian ridgeback
95. Ibizian hound
(tie) Welsh terrier
(tie) Irish terrier
98. Boston terrier
(tie) Akita
100. Skye terrier
101. Norfolk terrier
(tie) Sealyham terrier
103. Pug
104. French bulldog
105. Brussels griffon
(tie) Maltese terrier
107. Italian greyhound
108. Chinese crested
109. Dandie Dinmont terrier
(tie) Vendeen
(tie) Tibetan terrier
(tie) Japanese Chin
(tie) Lakeland terrier
114. Old English sheepdog
115. Great Pyrenees
116. Scottish terrier
(tie) Saint Bernard
118. English bull terrier
119. Chihuahua
120. Lhasa apso
121. Bull mastiff
122. Shih tzu
123. Basset hound
124. Mastiff
(tie) Beagle
126. Pekingese
127. Bloodhound
128. Borzoi
129. Chow chow
130. Bulldog
131. Basenji
132. Afghan hound

GIRLS LIKE TO BE PAWED BY FOOTBALL HEROES!

SPORTS STARS CAN CHASE DOWN MOST COEDS IN 4 SECONDS FLAT!

Stupid new study says college athletes are sex maniacs!

I'm madder than a gay football hero on a date with the Homecoming Queen about a stupid new report that says male athletes are about a thousand times more likely to commit "sexual assaults" on campus than dweebs, nerds, and bookworms.

Well, big bleeping surprise!

It doesn't take a nuclear physicist to figure out that pretty gals are more likely to tease and flirt with hunky football players than 98-pound weaklings.

And let's face it. These big-boobed, 10-year-old bimbos oughta know by now that if you wear skirts cut up to your panties, you're going to attract baseball, football, and basketball players like flies to honey.

And even if there are none of these real jocks around, you've always got wrestlers, swimmers, and track stars to worry about.

Everybody knows that nerds with Coke-bottle glasses have about as much testosterone as Liberace and are a lot more interested in the computer Internet than in net stockings. So who the hell is going to paw at the pretty little things on campus if the jocks don't do it? The professors? Gimme a break.

One thing's for sure—if we didn't expect athletes to have more sex than anybody else, we wouldn't tempt them all the time. We don't even let 'em have a minute to NOT think about all those sweet young things. Even while they're playing the game, we've got jibbly cheerleaders bouncing up and down on the sidelines, for crying out loud.

Hell, if I had to watch those babes strutting around for two and a half hours, I wouldn't care who won the damn game. I'd be thinking about getting my mitts where they don't belong, too—and I'm 65 years old, by jiminy.

So think about how you'd react if you were 20. You'd go after the girls the way my bull terrier Dodger goes after females in heat. And that means chasing 'em down wherever they go—including their dormitory rooms, if necessary. And guess what? Guess who catches the most babes on campus? The jocks, that's who. Why? Because they can run faster, stupid.

So just because they can actually run down and catch some squealing gal when nobody else can, the football star or the home run hero gets a rep as a sex pervert.

I'm just glad the Republicans are back in the driver's seat. I think maybe now we've heard the last of these bleeding-heart liberal "studies" that attack the very things that made this nation great—like baseball and football, by gum.

But what really worries me is, if enough athletes get scared off sex, where the hell are our little athletes of the future gonna come from?

Guess who catches the most babes on campus? The jocks, that's who. Why? Because they can run faster, stupid.

AFTER MUSHY MONARCH CALLS AMERICANS IGNORANT BUMPKINS...

Prince Charles gets an English lesson he'll NEVER FORGET!

I'm madder than Dumbo the Elephant with an earache over a comment made recently by that idiot Prince Charles of England.

This prissy, polo-playing potentate says that Brits speak the only proper English and that Americans are ignorant bumpkins who have trashed the language.

"We must act now to ensure that English—and that, to my way of thinking, means English English—maintains its position as the world language well into the next century," sniffed the prince. "The illiterate Americans are well on their way to destroying our noble language by creating bogus words and phrases and misusing those that already exist."

Well, excuuuuuse me, you flap-eared, horse-faced imbecile.

The truth is, the only Brit I've ever been able to understand was the late, great funnyman Benny Hill—and I only caught about every third word out of his mouth, for crying out loud.

In plain English, folks, people from England, Ireland, and Scotland talk gibberish. I'd rather listen to a bunch of Pakistanis in an elevator, by gum. I'd understand a lot more, for one thing—and I wouldn't have to hold my nose, for another.

If the Brits can talk so damn good, why the hell don't they tell each other to take a bath once in a while?

Hey, I've got nothing against the British people. We settled all that back in 1776 when General George Washington sent the Redcoat cowards scampering back to London with their kilts flapping in the breeze.

But if you think some Irishman with a fifth of whiskey under his belt can speak better English than yours truly, you're crazy. And as we all know, most Irishmen talk drunk most of the time.

And if you can understand ANYTHING anybody from Scotland says, you're a goldurned

Those English people talk like they've got a mouth full of **crumpets**, for Pete's sake!

Royal stink: Prince Charles finds OUR language repulsive.

genius. Whatever the Scots paid for English lessons way back when, they oughta get their money back, if you ask me. They talk like they've got a mouth full of crumpets, for Pete's sake.

Now I know why the Scots invented Scotch tape—so they could put it over each other's lips and not have to listen to the way they're butchering the language.

But what makes me so pig-biting mad is this sissy Prince Charles accusing us of making up words. Sounds to me like he's ticked off because the Brits aren't smart enough to add a little bit to their language now and then.

American is the only true English for my money—and I prefer how they speak it in the South over all the rest.

And I'll bet you a dollar to doughnuts that when the King of England greets somebody a few hundred years from now, he'll stick out his hand and say, "Howdy, y'all."

Newspapers around the world reported that Prince Charles attacked Americans' English.

Future English monarchs will probably learn to speak English as good as the rest of us.

Ed Anger

WHY ARE DEMOCRATS' DAUGHTERS <u>SO UGLY?</u>

I used to say about my plug-ugly Aunt Gert that if she had one more wrinkle, she could screw her hat on. But old Gert couldn't hold a candle in the ugly duck department to the daughters of our big shot Democrats over the last few years!

I thought Amy Carter was the ugliest Democratic First Daughter to come along since Lynda Bird Johnson, for crying out loud.

But Lynda Bird Johnson had an excuse for her ug-g-g-g-g-g-g-ly mug—she took after her dad LBJ, for crying out loud.

And Lyndon's picking her up by the ears when she was a little girl didn't help one bit, you can be sure.

Even my favorite president of all time—Harry S. Truman—had an ugly daughter. Margaret Truman looked like a tadpole, for Pete's sake. Her face wouldn't have stopped a clock, but it'd sure play hell with wristwatches.

And the late, great FDR had another coyote ugly daughter. Anna Roosevelt was so hard to take they had to tie a pork chop around her neck to get the dog to play with her. Of course, having that prune-face Eleanor as a mother didn't help. That gal was so ugly she could snag lightnin'.

Like my Uncle O.V. Potter's favorite saying, "Beauty's skin deep but ugly cuts right to the bone."

Remember those two Dukakis daughters, Kara and Andrea? They were so ugly the cat wouldn't look 'em in the eye. We're talking pig-belly ugly here, folks. These mugs not only could crack a mirror, they would peel the enamel off a refrigerator, for crying out loud.

Even JFK's daughter Caroline was no prize. But you have to remember that mom Jackie's eyes were so wide apart she looked like a catfish if you caught her head-on. Caroline took after her mother's side—except she also had a figure just like her grandfather Joe.

And let's face it, Walter Mondale's daughter Eleanor couldn't have won third place in a Miss Hog calling contest. She'd have scared a bulldog off a meat truck. But what the stupid Democrats don't seem to see is that every time the Republicans beat them to the White House, there's a pretty First Daughter!

Now Bill and Hillary Clinton's young daughter Chelsea is the prettiest would-be Democratic First Daughter in 40 years—but she's no Tricia Nixon.

Kinda makes you stop and think, doesn't it?

THEY MAKE REPUBLICAN WOMEN LOOK LIKE MOVIE STARS!

Like mothers, like daughters. They're all ugly, says Ed.

WATZ RONG WiTH americas' SCOOLS

I'm madder than a high school graduate trying to read a newspaper over something I just got in the mail from a teacher in Los Angeles.

"Dear Mr. Anger," she writes. "I'm a 12th grade math teacher in the Los Angeles public school system. For 13 years, I've tried with all my heart to give the kids in my classes the best education possible.

"And what do I get in return? I get punched, cursed out, mugged, constantly threatened, spit on, and laughed at by today's 'students.'

"But when I received this 'math competency test' last week, I finally broke down. When I refused to give this exam to my classes, I was fired for insubordination.

"But if this test is what our American public school system has come to, I'm glad to be out of it.

"Would you please publish this in your column so your millions of readers will know what's going on in our schools?"

Signed: A teacher who used to care, Los Angeles, Calif.

Folks, I'm so pig-biting mad over this, I'm at a loss for words.

Here's the test that drove this courageous teacher out of public education.

LOS ANGELES HIGH SCHOOL MATH PROFICIENCY EXAM

NAME:_____

DATE:_____

CLASS:_____

1. Johnny has an AK47 with an 80-round clip. If he misses six out of eight shots and shoots ten times at each drive-by shooting, how many drive-by shootings can be attempted before he has to reload?

2. Paul has two ounces of cocaine and he sells ten grams to Jackson for $820, and two grams to Billy for $85 per gram. What is the street value of the balance of the cocaine if he doesn't cut it?

3. Willie gets $200 for stealing a BMW, $50 for a Chevy, and $100 for a 4x4. If he has stolen two BMWs and three 4x4s, how many Chevys will he have to steal to make $800?

4. If the contents of an average can of spray paint covers 22 square feet and the average letter is 8 square feet, how many letters can a teenager spray with 8 cans of paint?

5. Hector got six girls in his gang pregnant. There are 27 girls in the gang. What percentage of girls in the gang has Hector knocked up?

6. Kathy gets $125 for sneaking an illegal alien across the border from Mexico. She sneaked three illegals over the border every night for six days but then one of them ripped her off for $500. How much money does she have left?

7. Byron can trade $150 worth of food stamps for two tickets to a Lakers regular season game. If a play-off game costs 20 percent more, how many play-off tickets can he get for $500 in food stamps?

ANIMAL ACTIVISTS ARE AT IT AGAIN, SEZ ED

I'm madder than my bull terrier at a cat show over that bunch of nincompoop animal lovers who want to outlaw the term "pet."

That's right, folks! These fruitcakes say calling your dog or cat a pet is insensitive and you oughta call them "companion animals."

"To call an animal with whom you share your life a 'pet' is reminiscent of men's magazines where you have the Pet of the Month," sniffed Humane Society bigwig Michael Fox.

And that's not all. Instead of calling all us pet owners "masters," these wackos want to call us "human companions of the non-human companions."

Well, excuuuuuuuuuse me!

If I called my dog Dodger a companion animal to his face, he'd bite the hell out of me, for crying out loud!

He's a pet and that's exactly what he wants to be called. And not only that, he loves to be petted.

It just goes to show you what our great country is coming to when you can't call a pet a pet, for Pete's sake.

But what makes me so pig-biting mad is that our children are being influenced by these bleeding-heart liberal eggheads who come up with this kind of doggie doo-doo.

Any animal that eats food you buy in the supermarket or pet shop is just that—a pet!

Next thing you know we'll have "companion animal" shops or "companion animal" cemeteries popping up everywhere.

Hey, I like my dog more than my daughter-in-law, for crying out loud. But give me a break! I'm not going to start calling her a "companion lunatic."

When will the millions of weirdos out there stop trying to change the American language by forcing these wimpy terms down our throats?

If these nutcases really want to know the bottom line, here it is, by cracky:

The next time your pet bites the plumber in his privates, you think that pipe jockey's gonna sue your "companion animal?"

Not on your life.

He'll haul YOU into court and take everything you've got— everything but the kitchen sink and the pet food, of course.

YOU CAN'T EVEN CALL 'EM PETS ANYMORE! NOW THEY'RE... COMPANION ANIMALS!

ED'S PC DICTIONARY

Native American— Red Injuns who would still be living in tents and pounding tomtoms if Pilgrims hadn't come to America. But thanks to us, they now run reservation casinos that make them rich.

Mentally Challenged— Stupid. Like that Forrest Crump or Chump or whatever his name was.

Vertically Challenged— Short. Like midgets or dwarfs. Usually easy to beat up or intimidate.

Visually Impaired—Blind as a bat.

Physically Challenged— Crippled or born without something.

Ethnically Diverse—Mutts or mongrels. Fun to look at but not great for the human race, if you get my drift.

Homeless People—Bums. The only work these people do is make signs telling people what they'll do for food.

Gay Community—The only place where you'll find more fairies than the Brothers Grimm museum.

Flight Attendant—Flying waitress. Once a gal had to be a babe to get the job. Now we got some real widebodies up there, if you know what I mean.

Chairperson—A girl head of something or other. Most likely a lesbian.

Hyperactive Child—Brat.

Attention Deficit Disorder—Brat. Again.

Sexual Harassment— What flirty girls scream when they get snubbed.

THE ONLY GOOD SPACE ALIEN IS A <u>DEAD</u> SPACE ALIEN!

I'm madder than an astronaut who just dropped a moon rock on his toe about all the bleeding-heart junk mail *Weekly World News* has been receiving about that slippery space alien who was captured— and then escaped a few weeks ago.

After our exclusive story and photos on this blockbuster event, thousands of letters poured into the newsroom about how horrible it was that our government agents put this lightbulb head in handcuffs and hustled him off for questioning.

"We should have been nicer to him. He looked so gentle and harmless," wrote one crybaby from Chicago.

"I'm ashamed at how this poor space alien was treated—put in handcuffs and slapped around by the CIA," wrote another fruitcake from Baton Rouge.

Baloney! Let's face it, folks. Space aliens are ruthless—not the friendly rascals in that E.T. movie. The Japanese have known it for years.

Their space aliens are the real thing—flying lizards and slimy, scaly things with big teeth that gobble people up like popcorn, demolish skyscrapers with a swipe of their tails, and knock over cars with their feet, for Pete's sake.

Space aliens are ruthless—not like the friendly rascals in that E.T. movie.

This captured alien just happened to LOOK a little more human, that's all. But I'll guarantee you he was scouting Earth for a full-scale invasion.

Otherwise, why on Earth was he sneaking around in the Virginia mountains?

And I want all you blubbering, sniveling wimps out there who think we ought to be nice to space aliens to get my message loud and clear.

Space aliens oughta be swatted like houseflies the minute they're sighted. And any red-blooded American who turns tail and runs from 'em is a damn coward! If this escaped alien ends up in my backyard, I'll fill his fish face full of lead so fast his ray gun will never clear his holster!

The whole Anger family has been alerted that this alien is on the loose—and don't think we aren't keeping our eyes peeled, by jiminey.

The only good space alien is a dead space alien. Period.

A LETTER TO EARTH

I was shunned because I am different from you and your kind. I came here in love and peace, to share with you secrets and answers to the questions that, for centuries, have puzzled the minds of scholars, scientists, and doctors alike. But to listen to me is to look at me, which you will not do. You detest my appearance. Call me names that cut through me like a knife. You think that, to be alien, I will not be hurt by cruel remarks. Well, you are wrong. I was given the same heart, the same feelings that you possess, and they were injured in the same way your's would have been, had I been you, and had you been me.

I was told that you were not ready, but I was willing to give you a chance anyway. I was wrong. I pray that time heals you, so that, when another of my species comes to assist you, you will greet him with open arms and accept him. Until then you must go on living like you have, with questions, doubts, wonder, and fear.

ENJOY THE CHRIST IN CHRISTMAS, ESPECIALLY YOU, MISTER ANGER,

PUT THE WALL BACK UP!

...AND KEEP THOSE NAZIS WHERE THEY BELONG.

I'm so mad I could pop my doc's blood pressure cuff that they knocked down the Berlin Wall over there in Germany—and that good-hearted Americans fell for this scheme.

As if we didn't have enough problems, now we've let those goose-stepping, beer-guzzling, strudel eaters get back together again. Great!

Now all we have to do is figure out which country we're going to let them invade after they get bored with the oompah bands and sauerkraut parties.

Let's face it. Germans have never really liked living in their own country. They're always trying to live somewhere else like Poland and France and Czechoslovakia—and the list goes on and on. I was worried that the Japanese were snapping up all the world's prime real estate.

But at least they pay market price for it.

The only offer the Germans ever made for a piece of property came out of the barrel of a cannon.

I mean, what if they come over here and say "Vee vont Disney Vorld."

We'd have to blast 'em back to the Rhine to keep them from shelling the daylights out of Cinderella's Castle and surrounding Mr. Toad's Wild Ride with storm troopers.

If those cabbage heads had their way, next time you took the kids to see Mickey Mouse you'd pay for tickets in marks instead of dollars. Donald Duck would be a Nazi and Winnie the Pooh would be in a concentration camp!

You know how I feel about the sneaky Russians. But they did the world a favor in August 1961 when they held the ground-breaking ceremony for the Berlin Wall.

They knew what I said about the Germans always wanting to live somewhere else was right. The Wall just fooled 'em into climbing over it and THINKING they were somewhere else! But what's really got me bouncing off the wall is all the liberal, bleeding-heart newspapers blubbering about how great it is that this "fairy-tale country" that gave us "Hansel and Gretel" is back together again.

Hogwash!

Germany gave us fairy tales all right—but it also gave us Adolf Hitler and those stupid-looking Volkswagens.

So when we're all eating Wiener schnitzel, don't tell me I didn't tell you so.

The Wall oughta go back up pronto—and I'll lay the first brick!

> When we're all eating Wiener schnitzel, don't tell me I didn't tell you so.

COLLEGE PANTY RAIDS ARE BACK—GOD BLESS AMERICA!

I'm madder than Hillary Clinton at a travel agents' convention over all the criticism our great college kids are taking these days.

You might find a hippie or two crawling out of the ivy on some campuses now and then but business classes are busting at the seams.

These fine youngsters are learning what this great nation is all about—the Almighty Dollar.

Even the late, great General George Washington sold junk bonds to pay for guns to blast those tinhorn Redcoats back to fancy-schmancy Buckingham Palace.

Let's face it. Most moms and dads struggle to send junior off to college for one reason—to learn to make money so they won't have to foot the bill for some pathetic 30-year-old-bum.

And girls go to college to meet these sharp young men who know how to make a fast buck. The true spirit of going to college is back at last.

According to my latest statistics, panty raids on girls' dorms are up nearly 61 percent from 1984 and fast approaching the levels of the 1950s. Now that's something to give the old college cheer about!

Panty raids are as American as football and on some campuses, they've even created teams of fraternity men to compete in this fun sport. The team that grabs the most underwear on any particular raid gets a free keg of beer.

I'll take those delighted squeals coming from a girls' dorm over the sound of Commie protesters blubbering into bullhorns any day.

And another thing. Army ROTC is more popular than pep rallies on campus these days. What better way to teach the Future Young Business Men of America to protect all the things they'll be able to buy when they graduate?

The M-16 assault rifle they learn to use in ROTC is better than all the lawyers in town when it comes to guarding their money.

And instead of some stupid folk

Annette Funicello and Frankie Avalon are great role models for today's students.

singer carrying a guitar around the quadrangle these days, the kids are carrying those newfangled portable computers.

Burn a flag on campus these days and you're liable to get a Radio Shack laptop upside the head.

So here's a snappy Ed Anger salute to all you college kids...You're the future of a wheelin' and dealin' America!

BLEEDING-HEART MOVIES ABOUT INDIANS MAKE ME SICK

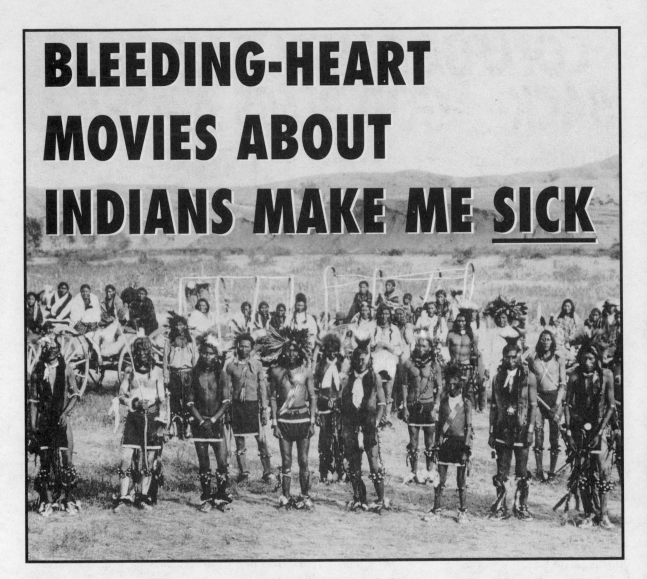

I'm madder than Hiawatha with a leaky canoe over all this Hollywood hulla-baloo about American Indians.

First of all, there ain't no such thing as an American Indian since America

didn't even exist before the Pilgrims came over and started calling it that!

But these weepy, bleeding-heart actors like Kevin Posner, or what-ever his name is, are always mak-ing movies that make the scream-ing redskins of the Old West look like really nice guys. Tell General George Armstrong Custer how nice those banshees were!

My wife Thelma Jean and I were watching those Oscar awards on TV a while back and both of us almost threw up when that injun movie "Taking Chances With Wolves" or some nutty title like that won picture of the year, for crying out loud.

That late, great Indian fighter John "Duke" Wayne must be spinning in his grave!

What about a film about those brave blue coats who killed Indians to make the prairie safe for the REAL Americans—those rough 'n ready settlers who tamed the West!

Hey, I like tom-tom music as much as the next guy, but give me a break. If I see one more peace pipe being passed around or some heap-big chief bellyaching about the white man's forked tongue, I think I'll puke.

Let's face it. We BOUGHT most of this great land from GREEDY Indians who'd rather wheel and deal for a fast string of beads than hunt buffalo. Manhattan Island in New York is a perfect example.

Indian real estate agents took the white man to the cleaners on that little deal—$24 for a few thousand acres of swampland. And 24 bucks was heap big money in those days, folks—about $340,000 in today's cash. And that kind of dough buys a lot of moccasins.

But what makes me so pig-biting mad is that if the Indians would have won we'd all be living in tepees, worshiping totem poles and reaching out and touching someone with smoke signals,

for Pete's sake. And another thing. I never heard an Indian on TV say much more than "UGH" or "HOW." But let one of 'em so much as grunt in these bleeding-heart movies and some translator says, "Chief Pain In the Butt says Great White Spirit blah, blah, blah, blah, blah," and goes on to recite the darn Preamble to the Constitution.

And all the Big Chief did was burp.

If those redskins were so great why do kids fight over who's going to wear the boots and six-guns in cowboys and Indians?

So let's put the movie Indians back where they belong—eatin' lead from Hopalong Cassidy, Gene Autry, and Roy Rogers, by gum!

If those redskins were so great, why do kids **fight** over who's going to wear the boots and six-guns in Cowboys and Indians?

LET'S PUT A LOCK ON U.S. BORDERS NOW!

I'm madder than a Mexican with his shirt caught on barbed wire over the flood of immigrants pouring over America's borders.

I know you sniveling, bleeding-heart liberals out there are going to pitch a hissy fit over what I'm going to say, but fasten your seat belts, buckaroos!

When my Anger ancestors landed on these shores back in 1773, they rolled up their sleeves and went to work the same day they arrived, by gum. They went to work because they wanted to eat.

And they didn't have President Rodham around to mollycoddle 'em, for Pete's sake.

But what makes me so pig-biting mad about today's immigrants is that most of 'em have tried for about a thousand years to govern, feed, and clothe themselves and still don't have a clue how to do it.

ED'S MADDER THAN HELL!

Let's face it. Immigrants in the early days didn't destroy their home countries before coming here. England, France, Germany, and Italy still operate pretty good, don't they?

That's more than you can say for Haiti, Mexico, South America, Pakistan, India, and all the rest of those two-bit countries that have been crippled by the same riffraff who are invading our shores as I write.

And not only that, most of 'em are coming here to see a doctor, for crying out loud! What in the hell are we supposed to do with nearly 234,000 AIDS-infected Haitians who'll land on Florida's beaches in the next year alone? Not to mention the dental work, by God!

Here's how the U.S.A. will look in 2010!

Carnegie-Atex ALERT!

This country's population of real Americans is declining at an **ALARMING** rate and our great nation is being colonized by hordes of Third World refugees in flip-flops. At the present rate of illegal immigration, the United States will be virtually over-run by the year 2010.

President Hillary can't even get decent health care for Americans and now she wants to jam-pack our hospitals with these people.

I'm mad as hell and I'm not going to take it anymore. CLOSE OUR BORDERS NOW!

And if you still aren't convinced, just take a gander at this quote from a recent Haitian refugee:

"Mother Hillary will take care of us. Americans are too rich, but Hillary will make them share everything with us and soon we will have lots of children to vote our will on the United States. This land will be our paradise, and if Americans don't like it, they can emigrate somewhere else like we did."

Like I said, folks...case closed.

DO YOU AGREE WITH ED?
ED ANGER IMMIGRANT POLL

☐ **YES:** I agree with Ed Anger that if we don't close our borders now, immigrants will overrun and destroy America.

☐ **NO:** Ed Anger is cruel and inhuman to attack free immigration, even if these poor people end up destroying our great country. It's a small price to pay to show we have a heart.

Mail your response to: IMMIGRANT POLL,
c/o Weekly World News,
600 S. East Coast Avenue, Lantana, Fla. 33462

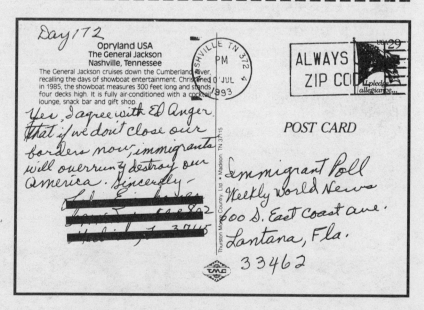

61

MAKE DOCS WHEEL & DEAL LIKE USED CAR SALESMEN!

I'm madder than a doctor with a dent in his Ferrari over all this crap about skyrocketing health care costs. Let's face it. The solution to this medical mess is easy as pie and would provide every American with top-dollar care.

Doctors and hospitals should do business like car dealerships, for Pete's sake.

Here are just a few examples of the way medicine oughta work under The Ed Anger Health Care Plan.

1. Every sawbones and every hospital should be forced to advertise in the classified section of the newspaper, right next to the those flashy new car ads:

This weekend only! Two Heart Bypasses for the Price of One! That's right, folks. Get your ticker in tip-top shape at Mad Mike's Surgery Outlet!

Super Doc can put you in a luxury double bypass for the low, low price of just $925.00—and a friend or relative gets one free!

Nurses, hospital gowns, anesthetic, and meals are optional. Second bypass must be done same day. No rain checks.

2. Doctors ought to go on the radio like those nutty stereo and tire salesmen:

Gotta Brain Tumor? Blown liver? Heart look like a hunk of lard? No problem. At Doctor Larry's Body Shop we'll have you running like a top in no time flat. Our factory-trained medical staff can get you back to being a party animal fast! Why be an invalid when you can throw away that wheelchair? We'll beat any competitor's price and we have the longest spinal surgery warranties in the business! Factory rebates of up to $5,000 on all transplants! We want to save, save, SAVE YOU MONEY!

3. Every hospital and doctor oughta have a staff of salesmen that greet you at the door with the hottest medical deals of the week. Then you could wheel and deal and get a rock-bottom price on big-buck operations like brain

EXCLUSIVE: ED ANGER'S PLAN TO CUT HEALTH CARE COSTS

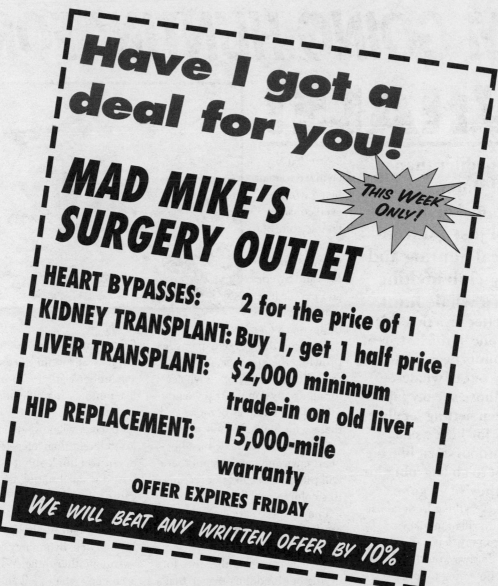

Have I got a deal for you!

MAD MIKE'S SURGERY OUTLET

THIS WEEK ONLY!

HEART BYPASSES: 2 for the price of 1

KIDNEY TRANSPLANT: Buy 1, get 1 half price

LIVER TRANSPLANT: $2,000 minimum trade-in on old liver

HIP REPLACEMENT: 15,000-mile warranty

OFFER EXPIRES FRIDAY

WE WILL BEAT ANY WRITTEN OFFER BY 10%

transplants and plastic surgery. These high-pressure salesmen could even duck out and check with the doctor if you won't budge on a price.

And you could start to walk out the door if they wouldn't take your final offer.

4. Every hospital should take organ trade-ins for transplants. A 40-year-old liver that was leaking bile might bring in a trade-in price of a thousand bucks, for instance.

A bum ticker should still be worth a few hundred bucks even with high mileage.

These trade-ins could be used for research or foisted off on poor people who can't afford any better.

5. Doctors and hospitals oughta have slogans like car dealers: "Bad Credit? No Job? Divorced? Noooooooo problem at Harry's Hospital Heaven—where nobody walks!"

Or "Sal's Discount Surgery—We cut for less!"

I'M GOING HUNTIN' FOR WHALE!

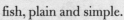

I'm madder than Daniel Boone with a rusty musket over a letter I just got from my local hunting and fishing club inviting me on a whale hunt.

The letter says that this will be one of the last great whale hunts because we're running out of whales. Seems those sneaky Japs have been netting 'em like shrimp, for Pete's sake! Now outdoorsmen like me have got to go bag a big 'un before they're all gone.

I've got everything from moose-heads to Brazilian monkeys mounted on my den wall and some whale jaws would look just great. So I'm going to fork over 1,800 smackers for a trip to some whale nests off the coast of California to harpoon one of these babies. But I'm still pig-biting mad that I have to rearrange my vacation schedule because we're running out of whales. All these countries who eat the damn things are to blame for the shortage, if you ask me.

Not that any civilized human being would even consider taking a bite of whale meat, by the way. But the Japs and Swedes and people like that will eat anything, that's for sure.

And with these greedy parasites prowling the open sea, it's going to be hell to find enough whales for all us guys on the trip. Nearly 50 had signed up as of today and that's a lot of whales, folks.

Now I know all those bleeding-heart environmentalists out there will pitch a hissy fit after reading this column.

They want to save everything on the planet—including the darned cockroaches!

A whale is just another fish, for crying out loud. Just bigger, that's all. My idiot daughter-in-law, Candy, is always blubbering about whales being mammals just like humans, but anybody who's ever seen one knows they're a fish, plain and simple.

If it swims in the ocean and can stay under water for more than five minutes at a time, it's a fish, by gum.

I mean a whale's not a heckuva lot different than a ten-ton flounder, if you think about it.

And whale hunting is not for gals or the faint hearted, either.

That late, great whale fisherman, Captain Ahab, lost a leg to Moby Dick, by jiminey.

And another thing. When there aren't any whales left and my little grandson, Teddy, is watching one on TV, I'll be able to tell him about how I bagged one of those big boys—back when men were still men!

GET 'EM WHILE YOU CAN BEFORE THE JAPS KILL 'EM ALL!

Let's hope foreign fishermen will save enough whales for the true hunters, says Ed.

ED'S WHALE POLL

☐ **YES:** I agree that Ed is pretty gutsy to go on this whale hunt and I hope he bags a big one.

☐ **NO:** Ed Anger should be harpooned in the butt for even thinking about killing a whale. I hope a big whale rams his boat and drowns everybody.

Clip and mail to: WHALE POLL, c/o Weekly World News, 600 S. East Coast Ave., Lantana, Fla. 33462

LET OUR KIDS BALANCE THE FEDERAL BUDGET...

IT'S NO SKIN OFF MY BUTT!

I'm madder than Ross Perot without a bar graph over all this baloney about balancing the federal budget.

Why in the world would any right-thinking American over 40 want to sacrifice the good life now so a bunch of people who aren't even alive yet can live it up sometime down the road?

I don't know about you folks, but I'm looking out for old Numero Uno on this one. That means ME, for those of you who don't speak Spanish—or chili pepperese, as we call it here in the Anger family.

Let's face it, I'd consider it tough love if we let the little brats and teenage delinquents of today work their butts off tomorrow to pay off the huge national debt that you and I are running up right now.

Paying off a big, fat national debt builds character, as far as I'm concerned.

So if today's teenyboppers end up having 50 percent or 60 percent of their salary withheld to pay off our national debt, great. It'll keep 'em from blowing their money on Michael Jackson albums, by gum.

And another thing. The Big Kahuna of this dumb-butt balanced budget crapola is that flap-eared Texas tycoon Ross Perot.

Hey, if I had a billion bucks in my bank account like he does, I'd make a hobby out of balancing the federal budget, too. Trouble is, most of us working stiffs are too busy trying to balance our own budgets.

And what greater gift could we pass on to future generations than knowing the value of the dollar?

Let 'em pay off a few trillion dollars of our national debt and I'll guarantee they'll know the value of a goldurned penny for that matter.

But what makes me so pig-biting mad are all these crybabies who are trying to trick older folks into balancing the national checkbook for 'em.

Do they think the Baby Boomers were born yesterday?

Now I know why they call young Americans "Generation X." They're so stupid, X is the letter most of them sign their name with.

You gotta be doorknob dumb to even think that I'm going to spend my hard-earned money to get America's young spendthrifts out of this balanced budget mess. And that includes my own spoiled brats, Jimbo and Sarah Lee. If Americans want to balance the federal budget while I'm alive, they'll have to do it over my dead body, by jiminey.

Paying off a big fat national debt builds character!

Ed Anger

WHY I HATE $1 COINS

And you know what else, while I'm at it? I'm madder than Susan B. Anthony with PMS over the Treasury Department's crazy campaign to mint a new $1 coin. Remember back in 1979 when Jimmy Carter was President and those yappy women's libbers talked him into issuing a $1 coin to honor old Susan B., the legendary suffragette who got gals the vote by beating the bejesus out of any man who opposed her? Well, the damn dollar coins went over like lead balloons and we've still got about a hundred tons of 'em stacked up in the basement of Fort Knox because nobody will use them. Let's face it. If the federal government put a 200-pound lesbian on our last $1 coin, who are they gonna put on this one, Liberace?

ED ANGER'S BALANCED BUDGET POLL

☐ **YES:** I agree with Ed that older Americans shouldn't allow themselves to be tricked into balancing the federal budget in their sunset years. Let our children and grandchildren pay the piper.

☐ **NO:** Ed is a selfish idiot. It's his generation that got us into this mess to begin with—so let's not stick young Americans with a tab they didn't run up.

Clip and mail to: ED ANGER BALANCED BUDGET POLL, c/o Weekly World News, 600 S. East Coast Ave. Lantana, Fla. 33462

LET OUR VETERANS SMOKE!

I'm madder than a GI who had to walk a mile for a Camel over a stupid Veterans Administration hospital banning its old soldiers from smoking.

Holy mackerel! Back on Pork Chop Hill in Korea we lived on Old Golds, for crying out loud. The one thing we looked forward to other than letters from home was getting those free cartons of cigarettes from Uncle Sam every week.

I've been smoking since I was 12 years old and I'm fit as a fiddle. I haven't had a cold in 10 years, for Pete's sake.

I can still remember the pleasure of lighting up after one of those bloody battles against 10,000 screaming commies back in '52. Those late, great Chesterfield and Pall Mall commercials were right, by jiminy—so rich, so smooth, so satisfying!

And now some whining health nuts and whippersnapper doctors still wet behind the ears want these old war heroes to snuff their butts.

"To my way of looking at it, we went overseas and went through hell for our freedom," says smoker William Newby, a patient at this nincompoop hospital in Lexington, Kentucky, and a WW2 vet. "Now they're taking it away." Damn right!

But the idiots who run this hospital say the old soldiers who were gassed in the trenches in WW1, bled on the beaches of Normandy and Iwo Jima in WW2, and were chine-gunned to hell and back in Korea have to go outside to light up!

I'll tell you one thing, bubba. The day some 20-year-old VA nurse tells me I can't take a few drags off a Phillip Morris is the day yours truly sends his Silver Star for valor back to the U.S. Army, by God!

I still remember the fine old GI motto, "L.S.M.F.T! Lucky Strike Means Fine Tobacco."

We went to war and fought for the freedom to smoke and we're sure as hell not going to give it up without a fight.

And if I get wind of these old soldiers standing outside a VA hospital in the freezing cold just to have a smoke, yours truly is going to war once again.

But this time it won't be against the North Koreans. I'll have my sights set on the bumbling Veterans Administration bureaucrats in Washington, D.C.!

ED ANGER SMOKING POLL

☐ **YES:** I agree with Ed that old soldiers have every right to smoke in veterans hospitals across this great land they fought to preserve.

☐ **NO:** Old war heroes don't have any right to smoke and health nut doctors should make them stand outside in the cold to light up.

Clip and mail to: ED ANGER SMOKING POLL, c/o Weekly World News, 600 S. East Coast Ave., Lantana, Fla. 33462

COMPUTERS ARE TURNING OUR KIDS' BRAINS TO MUSH!

I'm madder than William Shakespeare with a leaky pen that those computer bigwigs and TV shysters are trying to cover up the bombshell results of a recent public school survey.

According to the latest Carnegie-Atex Survey, underwritten by Oxford University, kids who read ANYTHING on the printed page have higher IQs than those who don't.

Well, surprise, surprise, surprise as Gomer Pyle used to say on the old "Andy Griffith Show."

I could have told you that, for crying out loud.

Everybody knows that kids who watch TV and play with stupid computers all day are dumber than those who pick up a book once in a while—or even read the back of a cereal box, for that matter.

But what really makes me pig-biting mad about this whole thing is the part where the study found that children actually LOWER their intelligence by not reading!

"Children between the ages of 8 and l2 who watched TV up to four hours a day had IQs that were actually 8 to l0 points lower than when they were tested at the age of 6."

Great! Now we'll not only have a bunch of preteen nitwits running around but these pinheads will probably decide what we'll all be watching on TV in the year 2000. Don't be surprised if "Baywatch" becomes the longest running TV show in American history with these kinds of viewers.

The study also found that kids who read even one page of a book a week outperformed computer nerds and TV airheads by a substantial margin on standardized tests.

As one of America's most popular newspaper columnists, I must admit that I've read a few Classic Comics in my day to pass a test on some great book we were supposed dig through.

I made an A on my *Moby Dick* report using Classic Comics, for crying out loud.

That's why I say let's put comic books in the classroom to get kids to read. They can read *Superman* for all the hell I care.

But if this new study is right, reading comic books is the best brain exercise our kids could get.

First thing you know, the kids would get so smart they'd start reading real books again and we could throw their computers in the garbage can, since they'd be so bright they wouldn't need 'em.

There's this lady idiot in the office who brags all the time about how she can work a computer. That was until yours truly asked her: "If you're so smart, what the hell do you need a computer for?"

That shut her trap, pronto!

Let's face it. Why did God make trees if he didn't want us to use 'em for paper to print on so kids could learn to read? No reason, that's what.

Reading comic books is the best brain exercise our kids could get!

BAD MEWS FOR THE PRESIDENT'S CAT!

Socks is tearing the White House to shreds, for crumbs sake!

I'm madder than President Clinton after she found a *Playboy* **magazine hidden in Bill's room over a story I just read about Chelsea's cat Socks.**

High-level sources say the Clinton pet kitty has destroyed thousands of dollars worth of priceless antique furniture, paintings, china, and historical documents on display in the White House.

"The Thomas Jefferson love seat had to be restuffed for the first time since our third President bought it back in 1804. Socks had peed on it for months before finally clawing it to pieces," said a disgusted Clinton aide.

Now, I'm a dog man myself and I never liked cats because they're stupid. And if it weren't for those bleeding-heart animal lovers, Socks would have been turned into a nice fur hat for my wife, Thelma Jean, by now.

But at the very least, we should pull all of Socks' teeth out and declaw the little sucker before all our national treasures are ripped to shreds.

Hey, let's face it. This demon with whiskers deserves to gum baby food for the rest of his life after wee-weeing on Tom Jefferson's sofa.

And the sofa incident just scratches the surface, folks. Here are a few of the other things the First Cat has done:

- Chewed the corners

PULL HIS CLAWS AND TEETH OUT, SEZ ED!

off the Persian rug given to Abraham Lincoln by the King of Siam in 1860.

- Eaten three stars off the first American flag made by legendary seamstress Betsy Ross.

- Used Revolutionary war hero Paul Revere's wooden leg as a scratching post.

- Left President Clinton's bras and panties strewn all over the White House and chewed the toes out of Bill's lizard-skin bedroom slippers.

- Knocked over two $80,000 Tiffany lamps presented to President Woodrow Wilson by millionaire John D. Rockefeller in 1920—and smashed them to smithereens.

- Did poo-poo in the Empress of Japan's open purse during a state dinner hosted recently by the President and Mr. Clinton. According to several guests, the Empress was disgusted and sickened.

Remember that troublemaking cartoon cat Sylvester who's always trying to make a meal of Tweety Bird? Well, he's got nothing on Socks—and I say something ought to be done about the little devil before he pees away any more of the taxpayers' money.

Dear Mr Anger —
What kind of a sorry childhood did you have anyway? Do you have any idea how painful it is for a cat to be declawed? If a doctor tried to do that to a human he'd be thrown in jail! Have a heart, Ed!

Alva Kenosha, WI

PAY-PER-VIEW EVENT OF THE CENTURY!

VS.

Dodger Anger   *Socks Clinton*

Three rounds. No holds barred.
Eat your heart out, Don King!

Watch the fur fly!

IMMIGRANTS WANT TO BAN OUR STAR-SPANGLED BANNER

This is THE column I thought I'd never have to write and I'm so mad I could chew up a hand grenade and spit the pieces in somebody's face!

A group of immigrants is trying to change our National Anthem to "America the Beautiful," for crying out loud.

The National Committee for New American Immigrants says we should ditch "The Star-Spangled Banner" because it is hard for Haitians, Hispanics, and Asians to sing. Even Chinamen have trouble with it, they say, pronouncing it Splar-Splangled Blanner.

Let's face it. I could sing "The Star-Spangled Banner" from start to finish by the time I was 4 years old, by gum.

And if these immigrants can't learn to sing it, they're either brain-damaged or move their lips when they read! Speaking of brain damage, I've got a steel plate in my head as a souvenir of my trip to the battlefields of Korea in '52 and I can still sing the Anthem without missing a note.

The late, great hero Francis Scott Key must be twirling in his grave at this nincompoop idea.

And some immigrants object that "The Star-Spangled Banner" is a war song. But just how in the hell do these idiots think the real America got here in the first place? With swords and bullets, that's how!

Sure, America's beautiful. And that's a nice song. But to sing that before a big football game or championship boxing match would be stupid. Lines like "And crown thy good with brotherhood," are kind of silly to sing before a game where everybody is trying to beat the other guy's brains out. "Bombs bursting in air" and "Rockets' red glare" are a little more like it.

Let's face it. "America the Beautiful" is a wimpy song and to make that our National Anthem would be an insult to the brave men who fought and died for our great country.

And if these immigrants can't pronounce the words to our great "Star-Spangled Banner," that's too damn bad.

Let's send 'em home until they can sing it frontward and backward—then let 'em apply for citizenship like our ancestors did.

> Haitians, Hispanics, and Asians say song is too hard to sing!

72

I think any immigrant that comes to the US should first know how to talk and read English. And not aloud to buy a home or have a business until they're a US citizen.

—AM

Please forward the results of this poll to the President and Congress of the USA & hope they pay attention for a change.

—LW

Must be some of the LOW LEFT not to simply adore the most beautiful song I've ever heard. It really stirs my blood to hear it sung.

—FRC

Tradition is important. We have so little of it. We have had "it" always. "It" belongs to America—FREE-DOM and land of the brave.

—ST

STAR-SPANGLED BANNER POLL

☐ YES: I agree with Ed Anger that these freeloading immigrants who are flooding our shores have no right to say anything about our National Anthem and should go back where they came from.

☐ NO: Ed Anger is a bigoted old fool. These brave immigrants, who are flooding our shores and rapidly outnumbering Americans who've been here a while, have every right to demand a new National Anthem.

Clip and mail to: STAR-SPANGLED BANNER POLL, c/o Weekly World News, 600 S. East Coast Ave., Lantana, Fla. 33462

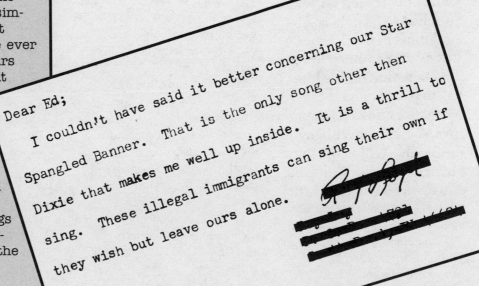

Dear Ed;

I couldn't have said it better concerning our Star Spangled Banner. That is the only song other then Dixie that makes me well up inside. It is a thrill to sing. These illegal immigrants can sing their own if they wish but leave ours alone.

GI JOE'S A HE-MAN TOY—NOT A DOLL!

I'm madder than a pit bull with a toothache that America's beloved toy soldier GI Joe has been officially branded a doll by those wimpy, nincompoop judges in Washington.

The only reason GI Joe even had to face those liberal idiots in black robes was over how much tax the company that makes him has to pay. You have to pay more taxes on dolls than toys, so those gavel-banging bozos gave GI Joe the same chance they gave Col. Ollie North—a snowball in hell!

But GI Joe will always be a toy soldier in the Anger household.

I remember buying my little son Jimbo his first GI Joe for his birthday in the summer of '74.

My chest swelled with pride when Jimbo dug a line of tiny foxholes across the front lawn and crawled GI Joe from one to the other for hours while making mortar and machine gun noises with his mouth.

His little sister Sarah Lee wasn't even allowed outside during Jimbo's war games with his GI Joe.

It just wasn't something a little girl should see, even if it was only make-believe.

Sarah Lee stayed inside and played with her beautiful Barbie doll collection.

My Uncle O.V. Potter says this GI Joe thing could get as nasty as flag-burning and it's already caused some firefights in our neighborhood.

My little buddy Butchy Hamorsky just got a GI Joe. Butchy is only 6 years old but he loves to come over on Saturday mornings, snap to attention, and say the Pledge of Allegiance in front of the flag on our front lawn.

Then he comes inside for some milk and pie and listens to me and Uncle O.V. Potter tell war stories.

Butchy loves playing with his new GI Joe and wants to be an Airborne Ranger when he grows up.

He can already beat the tar out of every kid on the block and a lot of them are a hell of a lot bigger than he is.

Uncle O.V. remembered the time Butchy knocked Mrs. Bern-ice Johnson's collie dog out cold when he was only 4 because the yappy thing wouldn't quit barking at him.

Butchy didn't get to come over last Saturday because his mom and dad had confined him to quarters for getting in trouble.

His older sister Wendy was teasing Butchy about how his GI Joe was really a doll and the next one he got would wet and cry until you changed its camouflaged diapers!

Let's face it, you might as well have called the late John "Duke" Wayne a fairy.

Butchy caught her with a karate chop to the nose and broke it in two places—and his sister is five years older and 20 pounds heavier than my little pal!

Uncle O.V. Potter has an old WW2 Victory Medal sitting on his dresser that we're going to pin on Butchy's chest when his parents set him free.

I'm with Uncle O.V. when he says that every little boy with a GI Joe should be just like Butchy.

If somebody calls your GI Joe a doll, waste 'em!

A newer verson of GI Joe perches on the arms of the original he-man toy produced by Hasbro 25 years ago.

...and Barbie is THE beauty standard for gals—no matter what those screaming women's libbers say!

I'm madder than a skunk in a perfume factory over this new fat doll toy-makers have come up with to challenge our beloved Barbie—America's plastic sweetheart since 1958.

That's the last thing we need, for crying out loud! A chubby role model for America's little girls.

What this new chunky doll does, folks, is tell girls it's okay to pig out whenever they want and end up looking like fat sows instead of Vanna White. This new "Happy To Be Me" doll is supposed to offer a "more realistic body image to young, impressionable girls." Egghead researchers say young gals develop eating disorders later in life trying to look like Barbie instead of some fatso doll.

Let's face it. Barbie is pretty and this new doll isn't. But what makes me so pig-biting mad is that the next thing they'll do is make this fat doll more realistic—and put plastic cellulite on her hips and thighs!

Barbie is, was, and always will be the ideal look for American women—not some corn-fed cutie with a behind broader than blubberbutt Oprah Winfrey's!

FRUITY VEGETARIANS WANT TO TAKE AWAY OUR RIGHT TO PIG OUT!

I'm madder than a pig at a barbecue at all those loony-tune vegetarians who're screaming their heads off for a ban on meat-eating in this great country of ours.

A gang of nearly 4,000 wild-eyed animal lovers stormed into the World Pork Expo in Des Moines squealing about how Americans shouldn't eat bacon, ham, or racks of ribs.

Then one of these ding-a-lings dressed in a pig suit charged the freshly crowned (and mighty pretty) Pork Queen and smacked her in the face with a non-dairy cream pie, for crying out loud!

If the good Lord didn't want us to eat pork chops, He wouldn't have given us humans sharp teeth, now would He? If these porker rights protesters get their way, we'll all be munching bananas and sunflower seeds. The backyard cookout is a basic American right passed down from the cavemen and the Indians who used to roam this great land.

Hey, I think baby piglets are as cute as buttons, but let's face it— NOBODY who gets a sniff of some juicy chops sizzling on the grill worries about how cute pigs

Ed Anger loves Porky Pig so much, he'd eat him in a minute!

are. All we care about is how they taste.

And what about the all-American tradition of the Christmas ham? If these bleeding-heart nincompoops have their way, we'll all be eating asparagus casseroles as the centerpiece of our holiday feasts.

But what makes me so pig-biting mad is that these hippie vegetarians aren't thrown in jail for hitting people with pies. If I were the judge, I'd give 'em 90 days on a hot dog and pig's feet diet, by jiminy!

When I was a boy, one of our favorite meals was hog brains and ketchup. In fact, Grandma Anger, God bless her soul, used to say that eating red meat and pork parts would make you smarter—and I'm living proof that she was right, by gum.

I still make it a point to eat a plate of pork at least twice a week whether I want it or not. I hate to say it, kids, but I'd eat Porky Pig himself in a heartbeat.

And if anybody's wondering,

the family sawbones tells me I'm as healthy as a horse—which is another thing I'd eat if one ever landed on my platter.

So let's keep that bacon sizzling and those pork chops frying.

And here's a little warning for those anti-meat fairies: Keep your little twinkie noses out of my backyard cookouts—or you'll be next on the Anger family barbecue spit!

ED ANGER'S
PORK POLL

☐ **YES:** I agree with Ed Anger that pork tastes good and it's our American right to eat it any time we want! And those vegetarian protesters should be thrown in jail.

☐ **NO:** The only pig that should end up on the grill is Ed Anger and anybody who eats pork is sick, sick, sick!

Clip and mail to: ED ANGER PORK POLL, c/o Weekly World News, 600 S. East Coast Ave., Lantana, Fla. 33462

KEEP WORLD CUP SOCCER OUT OF THE U.S.!

I'm madder than a little girl with mud on her dress about those sissy World Cup soccer games that start around the United States next month.

The games are being held in cities all over the nation and tickets are already on sale—but for the life of me, I can't imagine who would want one.

The only sport more boring than soccer is tiddlywinks—and at least in tiddlywinks, you have a chance to score, for Pete's sake.

Let's face it. No red-blooded American is going to sit around all afternoon and watch a game where a big score is 3 to 2.

Our pro footballers run up numbers like 27 to 14, and even that's nothing to write home about.

If the Chicago Bears played the Washington Redskins and the final score was 3 to 2, they'd be laughed right out of the stadium!

But the worst thing is that soccer's such a pansy game.

They don't have to wear helmets and pads like REAL American football players because they never hit each other hard enough to do any damage.

And the day the New York Giants take the field in short pants like soccer players wear is the day I figure the gays have taken over everything—including the National Football League!

The only sport that can be played in short pants and not be a sissy game is American basketball—and that's played indoors, mind you.

The only place you find any real action at a soccer game is in the stands. Soccer fans get so bored watching their favorite sport that they pick fights with each other just to liven things up.

And where are the cheerleaders at these nincompoop soccer games? Nowhere, that's where.

What they need to do is put a few babes on the sidelines like those Dallas Cowboys' cheerleaders and nobody would care that soccer's as boring as an artsy French movie.

Let's face it. England, France, and Germany sold those poor Third World sports fans a pig in a poke when they talked them into watching soccer.

But it's just like the late, great circus king, P.T. Barnum, once said, "There's a sucker born every minute." And it's a proven, historical fact that old P.T. was watching a soccer game when he said it!

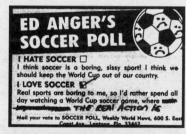

ED ANGER'S SOCCER POLL

I HATE SOCCER ☐
I think soccer is a boring, sissy sport! I think we should keep the World Cup out of our country.
I LOVE SOCCER ☑
Real sports are boring to me, so I'd rather spend all day watching a World Cup soccer game, where ~~nothing ever happens~~ THE REAL ACTION IS

Mail your vote to SOCCER POLL, Weekly World News, 600 S. East Coast Ave., Lantana, Fla. 33462

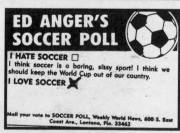

ED ANGER'S SOCCER POLL

I HATE SOCCER ☐
I think soccer is a boring, sissy sport! I think we should keep the World Cup out of our country.
I LOVE SOCCER ✗

Mail your vote to SOCCER POLL, Weekly World News, 600 S. East Coast Ave., Lantana, Fla. 33462

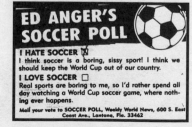

ED ANGER'S SOCCER POLL

I HATE SOCCER ☒
I think soccer is a boring, sissy sport! I think we should keep the World Cup out of our country.
I LOVE SOCCER ☐
Real sports are boring to me, so I'd rather spend all day watching a World Cup soccer game, where nothing ever happens.

Mail your vote to SOCCER POLL, Weekly World News, 600 S. East Coast Ave., Lantana, Fla. 33462

Handwritten letter (top)

Ed,

I agree with you 100% your ardicals are the greatest. You stick up for what most Americans belive not what the domonate media wants you to belive. Thanks for sticking up for what I belive in and keep writing about the stupid animal rights people. Its shows how wrong they are. But I have to confess something I am a member of P.E.T.A. I belong to "the people eating tasty anim[als?]". Keep writing those great ardicals your the greates[t]

A Fellow "Anger [?]"

[signature]

P.S. Soccer Really Sucks

ED:

Where and when did you crawl out from under your rock? In your next life I hope you come back as a soccer ball. If you were any kind of journalist, you would know how important soccer is to hundreds of millions of people. Did you know more people in the world play soccer than baseball and football combined? Your article is typical trash journalism, and you're writing on a subject that you obviously know nothing about. As usual, you are giving your personal opinions instead of facts. Do all us soccer fans and players a favor and change your job because you are no writer.

—GM

P.S. You probably have a lifetime pass to the badminton hall of fame.

Dear Ed A[?]

I usually en[joy?] [this sec]tion in the "Weekly World News," but when I read [someth]ing about soccer I screamed at the top of my lungs. When [som]ething makes me mad, I let people know about it. I won't send in the poll because underneath "I LOVE SOCCER" is an insult to all of us who love soccer.

I think soccer takes a lot more skill to master than say "football." All that you see at a football game is a bunch of jocks killing each other and fighting over a piece of pigskin! Very intelligent.

I am a redblooded American and I will watch a soccer game whenever I can. I'd rather clean the attic than watch a baseball or football game, who cares if they wear short pants? And they aren't short pants, they are called shorts, if you dindn't know that, you Dope! I don't see any difference between wearing shorts inside or outside, so what's your point with that Basketball bit?

So all I can say to you is: You really need to get a life, Man! I'd send you a penny to buy one, but you probably wouldn't want to take money from a "sissy," you twerp!!!

John H.

ED
WE LOVE SOCCER
YOU ARE A SICK MAN

GAYS BELONG IN THE ARMY, SEZ ED

World's greatest military heroes were limp-wristed pansies!

I'm madder than Davy Crockett watching a Mexican hat dance at the Alamo over all this hullabaloo about gays serving in the military!

Why not give the sissy boys a shot, for crying out loud? I don't care if they wear pink uniforms and roller-skate to the front lines as long as they get there and plug a few of the enemy.

That military genius Alexander the Great was so gay he decked out his horse in a lavender saddle and rhinestones—and won battle after battle for Greece back in the old days.

And Germany's famed Red Baron was rumored to be as gay as a $3 bill. But did that stop him from becoming the greatest ace in flying history during World War I with 80 confirmed kills?

And while he was playing hell in the skies over Europe, he even found time to set a fashion trend by being the first to wear those long silk scarves as an accessory to those trendy goggles and soft leather helmets.

And everybody knows that history's greatest soldier was a twinkletoes.

Lawrence of Arabia demanded that camels be color coordinated, for Pete's sake. More than one of Larry's troopers were executed on the spot for mixing a blonde camel with a brunette in one of his cavalry platoons.

And even the father of our country, George Washington, wore lipstick, makeup, and a powdered wig.

Check out an old portrait of Georgie Boy if you don't believe me.

And just who do you think designed those outrageous buckskins that Indian fighters used to wear? Pioneer king Daniel Boone, that's who! Danny was so gay he once stopped in mid-fight with a Cherokee chief to advise the redskin on his use of beads and feathers as a fashion statement.

And the list of gay war heroes goes on and on: Naval hero John Paul Jones, Confederate Gen. Robert E. Lee, Sgt. Alvin York of black and white movie fame…

And last but not least, Hans Felder, the interior decorator who died trying to scratch Adolf Hitler's eyes out while changing the color scheme in the Fuhrer's bunker.

If gays want to tote a rifle for the good old U.S. of A., I say let 'em, by gum!

Ed Anger

GAY SOLDIER POLL

☐ **YES:** I agree with Ed that gays should be able to be soldiers if they want to.

☐ **NO:** Gay people should be banned from being soldiers.

Clip and mail to: ED ANGER GAY SOLDIER POLL, c/o Weekly World News, 600 S. East Coast Ave., Lantana, Fla. 33462

80

INDIANS OUGHT TO WORSHIP CHRISTOPHER COLUMBUS AS A GREAT HERO, SAYS ED!

I'm madder than Christopher Columbus with a leak in his boat over all these bleeding-heart idiots who think old Chris was a bad guy!

And on the anniversary of his discovery of America in 1492, for crying out loud.

The metal plate in my head got hotter than a burner on Thelma Jean's stove the other day as I was watching one of the CNN interviews with those liberal eggheads Ted Turner slobbers over.

There was some mealy-mouth old broad on there and, if she'd had one more wrinkle, she would have screwed her hat on, for Pete's sake! Here's what old prune-face had to say:

"Christopher Columbus is one of the most evil men in the history of the world. If he hadn't opened up the New World, the Indians would be peacefully roaming their native land today—not to mention what the great Inca and Aztec societies would be by now if this cruel explorer had not opened the way for the Spanish Conquistadors."

Well, excuuuuuuuuse me!

What these noodle-brained Columbus bashers don't realize is that the great explorer SAVED the American Indians.

It's a historical fact that the Indians were bored out of their minds before the white man arrived.

Try living downwind from a buffalo herd for five hundred years, watching corn grow, and smoking a peace pipe now and then for kicks.

As for the Incas, they got so fed up with nothing going on that they started holding barbecues—with plump Aztecs on the menu. And when the Incas weren't eating the Aztecs, the Aztecs were eating the Incas, by jiminey.

Hey, so Columbus gave 'em syphilis. They gave us that stupid tomahawk chop that the Atlanta Braves and Kansas City Chiefs' fans do all the time, didn't they? So everybody's even, right?

And if Columbus hadn't discovered America, who in the hell do you think would have bought Manhattan Island from the Indians? That little deal put a lotta wampum in circulation, folks. And just who do you think would be jam-packing those reservation bingo halls and tax-free cigarette stores Indians like to run?

And what about those juicy mineral rights deals that put a new Ford Bronco in every Indian driveway?

Christopher Columbus is not only the first American hero—there wouldn't even be an American without him!

Believe it or not, out of these millions of natives old Chris found when he landed here, not one of 'em had thought up a name for the country.

They didn't call it anything. And that's after we gave 'em a couple of thousand years to come up with something catchy.

Columbus had to come up with it on the spur of the moment when his men asked him where they were. "America," he said. And the rest is history.

> **Indians were bored stiff until Columbus came and pumped some life into their country!**

RAISE THE PRICE OF AIRLINE TICKETS

I'm madder than the Wright Brothers with a busted propeller at how dirty and low-class flying on a commercial airplane has become in the last few years.

I just flew from Florida to New York and I had to use every barf bag in sight—and it wasn't the air turbulence that made me throw up, either. It was the fat, filthy old bag lady wedged into the seat next to me that made me sicker than a dog. The woman smelled like the inside of a Dempsey Dumpster in the alley behind a seafood restaurant, for crying out loud.

She couldn't afford to buy a bar of soap, but she sure as hell could buy a dirt-cheap ticket on a jet and sit down beside yours truly for the longest two hours and 20 minutes of my life.

Whatever happened to the good old days when flying coach was like flying first class today? Back then, passengers on jetliners were high-class, well-dressed folks you felt privileged to travel with. But those days are gone forever, my friend. A financial report just released by one major air carrier notes that the airline spent more money on upholstery cleaner than it did on jet fuel, for Pete's sake. That gives you a pretty good clue as to what kind of filthy, low-class folks they're packing those jetliners with these days.

And another thing. Those pretty stewardesses who used to wait on airline passengers hand and foot have been replaced by gals so ugly even the most nearsighted pilot won't invite them into the cockpit—even if they could waddle through the door. Sure, you don't have to pay chubby stews as much, but give me a break. When they're so broad across the beam and they have to walk down the aisle sideways, service suffers.

Hell, I waited 35 minutes for a beer while my stewardess stood wedged between two seats in the back of the plane, squirming to get out. It took two of those sissy male attendants to finally pull her free. Why in the world do I want to get on a plane and look at some dog-faced stewardess for two hours when I have my plug-ugly daughter-in-law Candy to look at every day of the week?

But the last straw came when a long-haired hippie sitting one row up from me paid for a cocktail with food stamps. I say up the price of airline tickets to where they used to be—high enough that the riffraff can't afford them. That way we'll put the trash back where they belong—on the bus!

...to keep the RIFFRAFF off the planes!

82

POSTCARDS FROM THE ROAD

NEW YORK: If you don't think the Indians got revenge on the white man when they peddled Manhattan's land to us for 24 smackeroos, just visit New York, the **ARMPIT** of this great country.

EPCOT: You can take a trip around the world and **NEVER SEE A FOREIGNER!** And you don't have to visit any undesirable countries like France—spend a couple of days in Paris and you'll know why the Germans really got the hell out of there at the end of WWII.

NEW ORLEANS: Settled by a bunch of **SWISHY CHEFS**. The booze was great but the food is for the birds—let's face it. You could be eating a dead rat in those fancy-schmancy joints and never know it because the corpse would be covered with sauce!

WASHINGTON, DC: Home sweet home to those **IDIOTS** we call Senators and Congressmen.

Miami: Anyone who goes there and isn't well-armed is crazy—you can't afford not to be prepared for an attack by one of the millions of criminal **LUNATICS** roaming South Florida.

LET'S DROP AN A-BOMB ON FRANCE

I'm madder than a Frenchman who's forced to use deodorant over all this hullabaloo about France resuming nuclear testing in the South Pacific. Now as far as I'm concerned, the Frenchies can bomb those Polynesian islands until they glow in the dark with radioactivity. If you've seen one hula dancer shakin' her booty at a pig roast, you've seen 'em all, I say.

But what galls the hell out of me is the way the most cowardly country on the face of God's green Earth is thumbing its nose at world opinion. Did you know that eight out of 10 French soldiers wounded in World War II were shot in the

butt? The only thing the French army has ever been best at is turning tail and running in the face of danger.

Hey, if anybody needs to keep building atomic bombs, it's France—because if you expect the French people to fight for their country, you're as loony as that frog-loving Bill Clinton. The only thing a Frenchman will fight for is a bottle of cheap wine or one of those floppy artist's caps they're so crazy about.

But seriously, folks, I think France deserves more than a little slap on the wrist for this crap they're pulling. I say we drop an A-bomb on Paris with the Eiffel Tower as ground zero! Nothing big, mind you. Something on the order of that 3-ton firecracker we dropped in the Japs' laps at Hiroshima back in '45.

If we have guts enough to do it, I think we'll have heard the last of bombs going off in Bali Hai.

...AND KICK CALIFORNIA OUT OF THE UNION!

I'm madder than Newt Gingrich in a gay bar over all the bad news out of California these days.

If it's not Mexicans streaming across the border like termites, it's drive-by shootings and circus murder trials, if you remember the one I mean.

I think Americans should vote the whole damn state out of the Union, by gum. What the hell do we need with California, anyway? We've got another Disney-land in Florida and the Super Bowl champion Forty-Niners are a razor's edge away from a hush-hush move to Montreal.

In fact, instead of dropping an A-bomb on France, maybe we should just ship California and everything in it to Paris. It'd serve those damn Frenchies right.

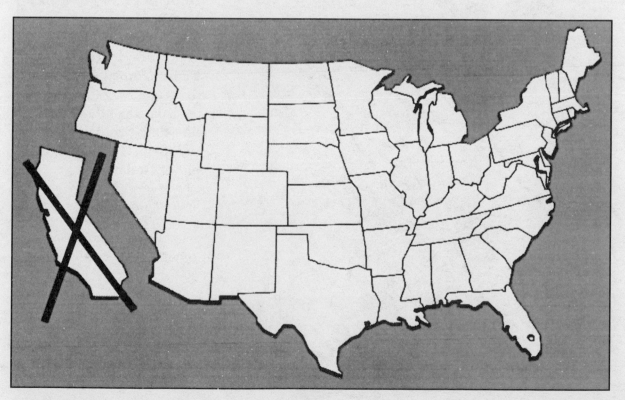

I'LL NEVER WATCH SPORTS ON TV AGAIN!

I'm happier than Babe Ruth with a case of beer that the boring old World Series is finally history.

I haven't watched an entire baseball game since Mickey Mantle was swatting homers for the Yankees in the '50s, by gum. And I'll be damned if I'm going to do anything to help pay the salaries of those million-dollar crybabies who call themselves baseball players today.

I don't even know who won this year's World Series—and I really don't care. It was just one army of mercenaries against another anyway, so who gives a

Today's athletes are a bunch of whining, overpaid SISSIES!

hoot who came out on top.

I remember the good old days when ballplayers were loyal to their teams and their cities and didn't jump ship just because another team offered them a few bucks more.

Back then, players loved the game so much they'd slide head-first into second base and eat a mouthful of dirt whether they took home a paycheck or not, by God. You can't even get today's sissies to run to second base without giving them some kind of incentive bonus or some such crap like that.

And the same goes for the National Football League. I won't even watch the Super Bowl this year—and that's a promise.

I'm sick and tired of not knowing a single player on my favorite team from one year to the next because they won't stick around long enough for anybody to learn who they are.

If today's pro football players want to play the game for money and nothing else, then yours truly has bought his last ticket. And watched his last Sunday game on the tube, for that matter!

And my wife Thelma Jean couldn't be happier. We're doing things on weekends like families used to. Like going on picnics and fishing trips and visiting the neighbors.

And furthermore, the National Basketball Association can go to Hell, as far as I'm concerned.

In fact, most of those guys aren't really as tall as they say they are—they're just sitting on

their wallets, folks.

And come on. If you were 7 feet tall, you wouldn't have much trouble dropping a ball through the basket, either. Let's raise the hoop to 30 feet and see how good these big babies are then.

Maybe if we all stop watching these so-called sports, they'll get back to the way God intended them to be—men playing great games for the glory rather than the moolah.

PRO WRESTLING IS THE GREATEST SPORT IN THE GOOD OLD USA!

Let's face it. Pro wrestling is what this great country is all about—kicking the bad guy's butt against all odds. And it's the one sport, other than boxing, of course, that the gays haven't infiltrated. There just isn't any such thing as a pansy-boy wrestler. These masters of disaster are real men who crush anyone who gets in their way—the kind of men America needs more of, in my book.

And they're the perfect heroes for our kids to look up to. I'd rather my little grandson Teddy practice choke holds on his playmates any day than learn to play piano like some sissy in a sequined suit. Which is exactly what he'd be doing if his mother had anything to say about it.

Candy says her schoolteacher brother told her pro wrestling is fake. I just wish that pencil-neck geek had guts enough to say that to MY face. I'd body slam the limp-wristed egghead so hard he wouldn't be able to add 2 and 2 for a week!

Most of those NBA guys aren't really as tall as they say they are—they're just sitting on their wallets, folks.

ED SEZ BRING BACK THE ELDORADO!

GET AMERICA ON THE ROAD BACK TO THE GOOD OLD DAYS!

I'm madder than Henry Ford in a Chevrolet over the sorry state of the Great American Automobile these days.

Every gol durned one of 'em looks exactly the same, for crying out loud, and goes about as fast as my Uncle O.V. Potter's riding lawn mower.

Those rolling tin boxes they make over in Russia have more style and muscle than today's stupid American autos.

That's why I say to hell with pollution control and gas mileage—let's get the machines that made this country great back on the road.

Here's the plan, folks. Since the last decent vehicle to roll off a Detroit assembly line was the 1959 Cadillac Eldorado, let's start making 'em again.

You heard me right, buckaroos. Let's make brand new 1959 cars!

All those egghead engineers in Motor City have to do is dust off the old blueprints for America's greatest road hogs—the 1952 Hudson Hornet, 1957 Chevy, 1958 T-Bird, 1959 Impala convertible, and so on.

If the stupid environmentalists start screaming bloody murder about some harmless exhaust fumes these big boys belch out, you could remake the only compact cars ever worth a damn—those dandy 1963 Chevy Corvairs and Ford Falcons!

And for all you nervous nellies out there worried about gas mileage, lighten up.

My sources in the Energy Department say America has enough oil to make plenty of high-test gas for the next 3 billion years. The sun will burn out before our gas pumps go dry, for crying out loud.

And another thing. Think about how much gas prices would fall. A brand-spanking new 1955 Buick, for instance, would get about 5 miles a gallon in the city and 12 m.p.g. screaming down the highway.

Using gas at this clip, the big oil companies would be pumping overtime to keep up with demand and prices would fall like lead balloons all over the country.

In fact, based on my supply side retro gas price theory, if we make enough brand new 1950s cars, gas prices should go back to what they were in the 1950s! How does 18 cents a gallon sound to you? Pretty good, huh?

Let's face it. Not only would these brand new 1950s cars sell like hotcakes to the Baby Boomers but wait'll Generation X gets a load of those double-bed-sized backseats and 185 m.p.h.

speedometers on these babies.

First thing you know, Drive-In Movies will begin to dot the great American countryside once again. Those old mom and pop Full Service Gas Stations will make a comeback and the shade-tree mechanics will do tune-ups the way God intended instead of some stupid computer.

Whole families will pile in these land yachts for Sunday drives, just like the summer of '56.

Try to get the whole family in one of today's cars and you'll suffocate one of the kids, for Pete's sake.

And try to get my tub-of-lard daughter-in-law Candy into a 1996 rolling sardine can and you'll get a hernia.

And another thing. These 1950s cars will give teenagers something to do besides drive-by shootings.

They'll go back to stealing hubcaps! Remember back in the 1950s when the worst thing teenage hoodlums did was pop off the garbage can lid-size hubcaps off cars?

Every car back then came equipped with hubcaps you could steal. It was sheer social genius on the part of the big auto companies.

Juvenile delinquents were so busy stealing hubcaps they didn't even have time to think about drugs. And besides, they quickly found that you couldn't steal as many of these shiny caps if you were drunk or high.

Let's start making brand new 1950s cars, and get America on the road back to the Good Old Days!

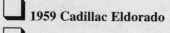

GOD'S REVENGE ON YUPPIES— CELLULAR PHONE CANCER!

I'm madder than Alexander Graham Bell getting put on hold over all this hullabaloo about cellular phones causing brain cancer.

That was after I was recently leaked a copy of a CIA medical report on the use of cellular phones as anti-spy weapons.

Of 27 former Soviet espionage agents who used cellular phones to do their work in the 1980s, 23 were dead by October 1990—of eardrum cancer that spread to the brain!

The report went on to say that the CIA sent Fidel Castro, Moammar Gadhafi, Ayatollah Khomeini, and Saddam Hussein cellular phones as anonymous gifts.

Only Khomeini used the thing on a regular basis—and guess what? Yep, he was dropped in his tracks by brain cancer.

But hey, there's always an up side to any deadly plague, right?

And in this case we're getting rid of all these yuppie creeps who sit at green lights yapping on their fancy phones like they were big shots or something.

And if you honk your horn at 'em, they just lift up their noses and stare down their antennas at you like rich people do when they see dog doo-doo on the sidewalk.

But you're damn sure seeing fewer and fewer of these cellular phone addicts on the streets. Cellular cancer is slowly but surely wiping out the yuppie class in this great nation, just like AIDS is doing to gays.

Now that may bring a smile to your face, but stop and think. How many God-fearing Americans are being bombarded with secondary cancer rays from these phones? God only knows, but one scientist likened the problem to secondary cigarette smoke causing lung cancer.

"Secondary cellular phone cancer rays penetrate even the thickest skulls up to 30 feet from where the thing is being used," this expert said. "If people must use a cellular phone, ask them to go outside or to a designated cellular area in public places like airports and hospitals."

The bottom line here is this. If you see a phone being used without a cord on it—run for your life!

And if you get a call from somebody using a cellular phone—don't answer it, for Pete's sake.

> **Cellular phone cancer is slowly but surely wiping out the yuppie class in this great nation!**

TODAY'S COLLEGES ARE SO-O-O EASY—EVEN ALFRED E. NEUMAN COULD GRADUATE, SAYS ED

I got madder than Albert Einstein with a busted calculator after a speech I made to some local college students a few days ago.

Yours truly had been asked by a professor friend of mine to tell 716 seniors how I pulled myself out of the Great Depression with a third-grade education to become the most talked about newspaper columnist in America.

Mad *magazine's dingbat mascot Alfred E. Neuman could pass any of today's college exams with ease!*

E.C. Publications © 1993

Let's face it. If you're looking for THE expert on pulling yourself up by your own bootstraps, I'm your man.

But all I heard after my inspirational speech was a bunch of 21-year-old brats whining about how tough things are these days. And not only that, they blame us older folks for screwing up the economy.

Well, I'm mad as hell and I'm not going to take it anymore. So listen up, you college pinheads!

Who the hell gave you the right to criticize the very people who built this great country?

And another thing, college has gotten so easy even John-John Kennedy got a law degree. So what do you REALLY think a college diploma is worth these days, you blockheads?

Well, I've created a little list that even you can understand. I've listed the college degree and then the jobs that particular degree best qualifies you for. Read it and weep.

Bachelor's Degree in Business Administration
French fry cook at Burger King or desk clerk at Days Inn.

Liberal Arts Degree
Nothing, unless you can get a job with a diaper delivery service.

Engineering Degree
Carpenter's helper. Plumber's helper. Welder's helper. Golf course maintenance.

Political Science Degree
Billboard erector. Telemarketing creep. Yellow Pages salesman.

Journalism Degree
Nothing.

Mathematics Degree
Assistant manager, Days Inn. Assistant manager, Arby's Roast Beef. President of one of those fly-by-night Florida cruise line companies.

Psychology Degree
Bartender. Waitress. Busboy. Parking lot attendant. Psychiatrist.

Graduate Degree
Tire recapper. College professor. House painter. Lawn maintenance. Poodle groomer.

And another thing, you spoiled fraternity and sorority good-for-nothings. The sooner you get off your fat butts and get one of these jobs, the sooner this great nation will be back on the road to prosperity—instead of the Highway to Hell!

LET'S DO MEDICAL EXPERIMENTS ON HUMANS

I'm madder than a monkey with a rotten banana over that AIDS guy who tried to cure his disgusting disease by getting a bone marrow transplant from a poor baboon!

In fact, I'm pig-biting mad about all these gut-turning medical experiments they're performing on innocent animals to make sleazeball humans well again.

I hope you caught that newspaper story recently about how scientists have discovered that animals have high moral standards, ethics, a sense of fair play, and distinct ideas about right and wrong.

In his blockbuster new book,

We can use criminals and illegal aliens as "human lab rats"—and infect 'em with dog & monkey viruses!

Good Natured: The Origins of Right and Wrong in Humans and Other Animals, Frans de Waal of Emory University says chimps share food, kiss and make up after fighting, and hug all the time to make each other feel better.

My English bull terriers Dodger and Blossom come up and lick me to make me feel better when I'm mad as hell and even fluff up my pillow at night before the wife and I turn in.

Blossom goes so far as to share

Lassie is more valuable than many human beings, says Ed.

Using baboon blood to help AIDS creeps is an OUTRAGE!

her food with my fat daughter-in-law Candy—who usually eats it, by the way.

And unlike some 2-year-olds I know, Blossom and Dodger know right from wrong and don't crap on the carpet.

Let's face it. I think it's high time we started injecting humans with animal diseases so Dodger and Blossom can live longer and healthier lives. Our prisons are full of "humans" we could infect with all kinds of animal diseases and then try to cure them.

In fact, we could even offer reduced sentences to cons who volunteer to let us make them sicker than a dog with animal diseases. And what about all those illegal aliens who'd like to make a little cash for a rainy day? Here's their chance, by jiminey.

The *Washington Post* recently reported that humans are routinely used as "lab rats" in China, Japan, and Malaysia to find cures for animal diseases, and especially canine diseases.

Everybody knows dog is as highly prized at the dinner table in Tokyo as T-bone steak is in Kansas City.

Last year alone, nearly 60,000 Japanese men, women and children gave their lives in an attempt to find cures for doggie diseases.

So, by gum, I think every veterinary college in America oughta start doing animal disease experiments on humans. Now.

Ed Anger

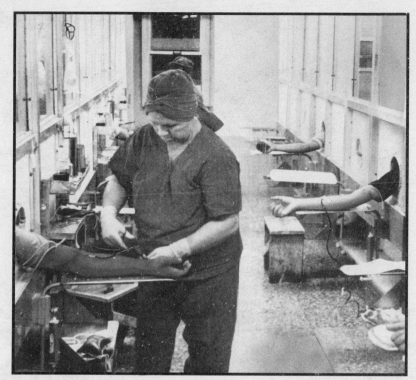

Human lab rats are injected with canine parvo—a disease that kills 40,000 dogs annually. Veterinarians in Mexico, where this photo was taken, hope to find a cure by experimenting on humans.

ED ANGER'S
LAB RAT POLL

☐ **YES:** I agree with Ed that we should start doing animal disease experiments on humans for a change. Criminals and illegal aliens would be perfect "lab rats" and they could earn a little rainy day cash at the same time.

☐ **NO:** You sicken me, Ed Anger! Even the lowest, vilest child molester is worth more in God's eyes than your loyal, valiant, loving dogs.

Clip and mail to: ED ANGER'S LAB RAT POLL, c/o Weekly World News, 600 S. East Coast Ave., Lantana, Fla. 33462

ED ON MEN: RULES FOR HENPECKED WALLY WUSSIES

1. Real men don't cry—and I mean not a whimper. I haven't cried since I was 3 years old and I ran out of BBs trying to kill a hummingbird.

2. Real men don't talk much. I haven't said 10 words to my wife in three weeks. Sentences should be no longer than "Get me a beer."

3. Real men don't do housework. That's the reason God gave women tiny hands—so they could clean in every nook and cranny.

4. Real men don't play golf. Any man who plays golf ought to have a sex-change operation.

5. Real men eat, drink, and smoke whatever they want, whenever they want.

6. Real men don't read *Playboy*. They don't read anything if they can help it.

7. Real men don't wear any cologne but Old Spice.

8. Real men don't go to the doctor—unless they croak and need a death certificate.

9. Real men don't say "I'm sorry." If you hurt somebody's feelings a little, forget about it. Even if they don't, it's no skin off your butt.

10. Real men burp—anywhere, anytime.

ED ON WOMEN: HEELS ON WHEELS

I think it's high time for our country to begin issuing a special WOMAN'S DRIVER'S LICENSE. Now before all you screaming women's libbers throw a big hissy fit, I'm not going to say we should ban all women from driving. I know that's probably a good idea, but the fact is, someone has to drive the kids to school and go to the store for groceries.

Before a woman could get one of these licenses, she'd have to take a test that includes some of the hairbrained stuff they like to do best—like using the rearview mirror to put on makeup while zipping through traffic at 60 m.p.h. They'd also have to show they can drive while holding a cigarette in one hand and adjusting a baby seat with the other.

And since women tend to get lost a lot and drive past their turnoffs, we oughta give them a special test for all the U-turns they're always making in the middle of the street. The WOMAN'S DRIVER'S LICENSE would be invalid during morning and evening rush hours so women drivers couldn't clog the roadways when men are hurrying to get to and from work. For heaven's sakes, that shouldn't bother them since they have the roads all to themselves eight hours a day while us men are working anyway. I'd even agree to leave all weights and ages off a WOMAN'S DRIVER'S LICENSE, since most gals like keeping information like that a big secret.

And while we're at it, we ought to give women their own special

lane to drive in. That way they can drive 20 m.p.h. with one foot on the brake and turn right with their left blinker flashing and even hang both hands out the window to dry their fingernail polish all day long. And no one behind them will get upset, because everybody in their lane would be doing the same dagblamed thing.

I'D RATHER LIVE NEXT TO A PRISON THAN A PUBLIC SCHOOL!

I'm madder than a math teacher with a busted calculator over what I just saw being built at the end of my street—a durned elementary school, that's what. Let's face it, folks. My neighborhood would be better off if they were building a penitentiary instead. I mean, everybody knows there are probably more criminals in our public schools than in our jails these days, for crayon' out loud. And at least the jails don't let all the rapists and murderers go home when the bell rings.

If a teacher so much as slaps one of these Future Scumbags of America on the wrist, they're suspended without pay and brought up on charges, for Pete's sake. And that's not all. Guess what happens to property values when one of these public holding pens for thieves and miniature crackheads goes up.

"When a public school goes up within a mile of your property, you can take 30 percent of your home's value and flush it down the toilet. People with any brains at all are not going to risk living anywhere near a public school in the 1990s. Period," says a recent report of the American Realtors and Contractors Association. To live near a public school is just asking for you or a member of your family to be murdered, robbed or maimed.

And folks, I'm mad as hell and I'm not going to take it anymore. I'm rallying my neighbors to stand in front of the bulldozers to stop this school from being built here. They can build a nuclear plant, an insane asylum or an AIDS hospital on the site and I won't say a damned word. But this public school stuff is going too far, by gum.

I didn't charge up Pork Chop Hill in Korea back in '52 to have some county school board threaten my life and liberty in 1993. If they finish this elementary school, it'll be over my dead body. And that's not a threat, Bubba, that's a promise.

My Garden of the Gods

ED ANGER

WITH PHOTOS!

THE INDUCTEES

JUDGE ROY BEAN. HE PASSED OUT DEATH SENTENCES LIKE MCDONALD'S SERVES BIG MACS!

page 98

TONYA HARDING. THIS THUNDERTHIGHED REDNECK ICE-SKATING QUEEN KICKS GLADIATOR BUTT!

page 98

MADONNA. THIS SINGIN' MOMMA'S HOTTER THAN A TWO-DOLLAR PISTOL, BY GUM!

page 98

EDWARD R. MURROW. HATS OFF TO THIS TOP-NOTCH NEWSMAN WHO WOULDN'TA BEEN CAUGHT DEAD WITHOUT A CIGARETTE!

page 99

RICHARD MILHOUS NIXON. THE GREATEST PRESIDENT WHO EVER LIVED.

page 99

OLLIE NORTH. LET'S PUT THIS HERO ON MT. RUSHMORE.

page 99

BERT PARKS. THIS LIVING LEGEND IS THE BEST THING THAT EVER HAP-PENED TO THE MISS AMERICA PAGEANT!

page 100

ROSS PEROT. HE'S GOT A STEEL-TRAP MIND AND A HEART AS BIG AS TEXAS!

page 100

JOHN "DUKE" WAYNE. THE MANLIEST MAN WHO EVER JINGLED IN A PAIR OF SPURS!

page 100

AND MORE...

JUDGE ROY BEAN

Judge Roy Bean, the late great hanging judge of Texas, who billed himself as "the law west of the Pecos" in the late 1800s. That tough ol' Judge Bean passed out death sentences like McDonald's passes out Big Macs. And he didn't need to pop a tranquilizer to throw these little necktie parties, either. The sick criminals who roam our streets today would be the ones having panic attacks if they landed in Judge Bean's courtroom. That's because the scumbags would be taking dancing lessons at the end of a rope by sundown. Now in all fairness, Judge Bean was rumored to have taken a shot of red-eye whiskey on occasion—but NEVER before showing up at one of those hell-raising gunslinger's trials. It took nerves of steel to stare those desperadoes in the eye and order them hanged by the neck until dead, by golly.

Tough Judge Roy Bean, played by Paul Newman

TONYA HARDING

Tonya Harding, the redneck ice-skating queen who had a couple of things going for her that Nancy Kerrigan didn't have—thighs like Emmitt Smith of the Dallas Cowboys and something in her skull besides air. Stupid, she ain't. In fact, she's one smart cookie—and a worker, too, by jiminey. She's already earned enough money to pay off the $100,000 fine she got for busting Nancy's leg. And she delivered food to the needy as part of the 500 hours of community service work the judge ordered her to do. AND this spunky little gal holds down a job with a landscaping firm, cutting grass and trimming hedges. And get this: After posing in *Esquire* magazine, all dolled up in a gold evening gown next to a truck, she went out and put those thunderthighs to work on American Gladiators, kicking a little gladiator butt. All this while little Miss Nancy "Nobody" is riding around on some dumb Disney World float acting dumb and picking up chump change with the Ice Capades, and while that beanpole Russian chick who won the Gold Medal doesn't have two rubles to rub together. God bless America.

MADONNA

Madonna. She may be the ultimate bimbo, but she's hotter than a two-dollar pistol in my book. I even keep a poster of her in my office, for crying out loud. The louder those old spinsters out there screech that Madonna is a slut, the more I like her. Put most of these Madonna-bashers in a thong bathing suit and the damned sharks would hightail it, for Pete's sake! I've said it before and I'll say it again: Madonna is the best thing to happen to showbiz in America since Marilyn Monroe. Hey, compared to that plastic-surgery-poster-boy Michael Jackson, Madonna is a breath of fresh air. And you sure as hell won't find her playing Post Office with little boys, either! I might be an old hepcat from the 1950s, but I still tune in to MTV at least two hours a day just waiting for a Madonna music video, so I know what I'm talking about. Madonna is the best girl singer since Patti Paige and I'm still one of her biggest fans—no matter what kind of book she takes her clothes off in.

EDWARD R. MURROW

Edward R. Murrow, the late great newsman who wouldn't have been caught dead without his cigarette. His prize-winning TV program "See It Now" wouldn't have been the same if he hadn't chain-smoked on every show, now would it? If the anti-smoking banshees had their way, Murrow would have munched on jelly beans instead of puffing on Lucky Strikes. He must be twirling in his grave over all those squealing, pencil-neck health freaks who want to snuff out the great American pastime of tobacco smoking!

RICHARD MILHOUS NIXON

Richard Milhous Nixon, the most courageous President of modern times. He battled the bleeding-heart liberals with an iron fist for near-ly fifty years. He stood on the front lines for the Silent Majority of Americans who know right from wrong. He might have been known as Tricky Dick back then, but he was tricky enough to keep America on a laser-beam course to prosperity and world respect. In other words, we all had plenty of cash in our pockets and our military scared the bejesus out of every country on the planet! In your heart, you know he was right. The only BIG mistake he ever made was let-ting Slick Willie Clinton dodge the Vietnam draft. He was a great leader and a brilliant statesman. Dick Nixon was the best American President of this century and most historians are finally admitting it. Richard Nixon's head ought to be carved on Mt. Rushmore.

OLLIE NORTH

That some stupid liberal judge made the pride of the U.S. Marine Corps a convicted felon instead of putting his face on Mt. Rushmore makes my blood boil. The only thing the Colonel is guilty of is being the greatest patriot since General George Washington of Revolutionary War fame. But George got rewarded for his super courage after whipping a little Redcoat tail when the grateful American people made him First Prez of our new nation. When Ollie puts his butt on the line by tricking those sand-eating fruitcakes in Iran into giving guns and bullets to our freedom fighter friends South of the Border, those liberal fools in Washington make him a criminal who can't be President of this great nation. And to think he got a big fine instead of a Congressional Medal of Honor makes me pig-biting

mad. I say we change the law and let all criminals run for any office they want. We might get a few bad eggs running things for a while but we could put Ollie North in the Oval Office where he belongs.

BERT PARKS

Bert Parks, the best thing that ever happend to the Miss America contest. Nobody, and I mean nobody, sings "Here She Comes, Miss America" like good old Bert. He may have botched a few lines in the 1990 pageant—so what if he gets messed up and calls Miss Virginia Miss California and Miss Utah Miss Florida or so what if he walks onstage with toilet paper stuck to his shoe, for that matter. He's STILL tops in my book! A living legend like Bert Parks deserves one last shot at the Miss America shindig—and we ought to help him get it!

ROSS PEROT

He looks like Harry Truman, talks like Harry Truman, walks like Harry Truman, and if you believe in reincarnation, he just might be Harry Truman! What we've got here is the greatest American since George Washington. This guy pulled himself up by his own bootstraps from a dirtpoor childhood to life as a billionaire with a $100 million checking account. And he's never bounced a single check, by God. This is a guy with a steel-trap mind and a heart as big as his home state of Texas. And I'd bet my war medals that he could have done just what he said if he was our commander-in-chief—put America back to work, lower taxes, feed the hungry, whip the Japs at business, boot those lazy fatcats out of Congress and make our great country No. 1 again, by gum. It's a shame Cheatin' Bill Clinton stole the election.

JOHN "DUKE" WAYNE

John "Duke" Wayne, maybe the manliest man who ever jingled in a pair of spurs. The guy walked like man, talked like a man, sweat and spit like a man—he was the ideal American male. Some limp-wristed French guy tried to suggest that the Duke was homosexual, but I and every other God-fearing American know THAT is a crock of crap. We know John Wayne was straight as a long, dusty highway because a homosexual tried to date him once and the Duke gave him a lecture with his right fist. That's my idea of setting the record straight. The only big mistake he ever made was not running for President of this great country.

My Hall of Shame

ED ANGER

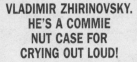

WITH PHOTOS!

THE INDUCTEES

ROSEANNE BARR-F. SHE HUMILIATED OUR FLAG!
page 102

BATBOY. HE'S MEAN AS THE DICKENS, AND HE AIN'T STUPID!
page 102

CANDACE BERGEN. HER BROTHER WAS A DUMMY NAMED MORTIMER SNERD, FOR CRYING OUT LOUD!
page 102

FIDEL CASTRO. THE REAL CASTRO'S DEAD AS A DOOR KNOB!
page 103

HILLARY RODHAM CLINTON. HER COTTON-PICKING COOKIES TASTE LIKE DOG BISCUITS!
page 103

LEONA HELMSLEY. THAT PORKY FAT-CAT LOUNGES AROUND EATING CAVIAR AT OUR EXPENSE!
page 104

SADDAM HUSSEIN. WE SHOULD BLOW THAT TOWEL-HEADED TYRANT AWAY FOR GOOD!
page 104

THE U.S. SENATE WITHOUT TEDDY WOULD BE LIKE CUBA WITHOUT CASTRO!
page 105

JACKIE KENNEDY. SHE'S NO DOLLY MADISON!
page 105

ROSS PEROT. THIS GUY COULDN'T RUN A WASHING MACHINE MUCH LESS OUR GREAT COUNTRY!
page 106

O.J. SIMPSON. LET'S EXECUTE HIM AT SUPER-BOWL HALFTIME!!
page 106

VLADIMIR ZHIRINOVSKY. HE'S A COMMIE NUT CASE FOR CRYING OUT LOUD!
page 107

AND MORE...

ROSEANNE BARR-F

She's famous for insulting every brave serviceman and veteran by butchering our country's national anthem before some baseball game. It makes my blood boil to think that I've got a metal plate in my head from the Korean War so this 300-pound bag of blubber is free to rake in $5 million a year from some idiotic TV comedy show. Of course, even that much money doesn't go far when you spend seventy grand a week on groceries. I mean, how'd you like to battle this foul-mouthed beach ball for the last pork chop on the dinner table? She humiliated our flag, our nation, our heritage, and the memory of every heroic American who died under "the rockets' red glare."

BATBOY

Batboy's the two-foot-tall demon with teeth like Gillette razor blades and a tongue like a Brillo pad that escaped from a high security research facility in West Virginia and remains at large. He's got eyes the size of ping-pong balls that let him find you in the dark and a set of ears as big as a small catcher's mitt. Scientists insist that this creature eats about 20 pounds of insects a day. Baloney! Look at the kid. If he runs out of bugs, miniature poodles start to look awfully tasty. He's as mean as the dickens and he ain't stupid. He may be the biggest threat to the U.S. since Hurricane Andrew and I'm going to keep my eyes peeled for this bat brat. I suggest you do the same.

CANDACE BERGEN

Candace Bergen, one of those sicko liberal actresses with an IQ just slightly higher than my bull terrier's! That's no big surprise, considering her brother was a wooden dummy named Mortimer Snerd, for crying out loud. And her dad Edgar pulled the greatest con job in the history of entertainment when he took his ventriloquist gig to radio. That made it harder for his listeners to see his big, fat lips move! I could be a damned ventriloquist on the radio, for Pete's sake. I've never seen that damned "Murphy Brown" on the boob tube, but the boys down at the Dew Drop Grill tell me it's a stupid program about some yuppie gal who likes to have babies without getting married—just the kind of godless behavior that's caused the breakdown of the American family, by gum.

FIDEL CASTRO

Fidel Castro, that wily old windbag who swore he'd rather eat grass than let McDonald's invade his island empire, but who gulped down Chicken McNuggets like popcorn and scarfed down Big Macs by the bushel behind closed doors. Three chefs disappeared after he ordered them to make hamburgers just like McDonald's and they never got it right! But that's neither here nor there because my high-level sources in the CIA tell me that the real Castro is dead—and has been since January 1991, when he dropped dead of a heart attack in his Havana apartment. The dingbat dictator is pushing up daisies in some burned-out sugarcane field. The Fidel who showed up at the United Nations a while back was a fake. I bet old Dan Rather feels foolish right now—what was that frequency? Heh-heh.

HILLARY RODHAM CLINTON

It takes a village, my butt. This woman won't stop until she's boss of the whole world. It's clear who wears the pants in the White House—and it ain't Slick Willie. The only thing Hillary's got that's presidential is a butt as wide as 360-pound William Howard Taft's.

   Hillary Rodham is a man-hater, by gum, and if she wasn't running the show in Washington, she'd be parading around with those motorcycle-riding, weight-lifting she-males in the National Organization for Women. And as if that isn't enough, she wants to invite every sick person on the whole damn planet to come here and take it easy on us hardworking taxpayers. Listen, I've baked a batch of Hillary Clinton's oatmeal chocolate chip cookies and now I see

THESE COTTON-PICKING THINGS TASTE LIKE DOG BISCUITS

HILLARY'S RECIPE

1 1/2 cups unsifted all-purpose flour	1 teaspoon salt
1 teaspoon baking soda	1 cup solid vegetable shortening
1/2 cup granulated sugar	1 cup firmly packed light brown sugar
1 teaspoon vanilla extract	2 eggs
2 cups rolled oats	12 ounces semisweet chocolate chips

Heat oven to 350 degrees. Combine flour, salt, and baking soda. Beat together shortening, sugars, and vanilla until creamy. Add eggs, beating until fluffy. Gradually beat in flour mixture and rolled oats.
Stir in chips.
Drop teaspoonfuls of batter onto cookie sheets. Bake 8 to 10 minutes. Cool cookies on sheets for two minutes before placing them on wire rack for further cooling. *Yield: A whole bunch of inedible cookies.*

why the lady became a lawyer. Those cotton-picking things taste like dog biscuits, for crying out loud! My little grandson Teddy took one nibble and immediately started banging his head on the floor. This woman's dangerous, I tell you—the sooner the voters of this great country convince her to go back where she came from, the better.

HOLLYWOOD BLEEDING HEARTS

Bleeding hearts like that whining liberal actress Susan Saranwrap and movie star boyfriend Tim Robbins, who pitch a hissy fit because we don't welcome foreign AIDS carriers into the United States with open arms—hey, if those two want to share their Beverly Hills mansion with 40 or 50 AIDS-infected Haitians, great! Or what about that big mouth movie star Richard Gere, who used the Academy Awards show to scream at the Red Chinese, for crying out loud, going into a tirade about how Chinese bosses don't know how to show love or some such crap. These sniveling left-wing show folks should rent a soap box if they want to preach their bleeding heart, mush-mouth drivel.

LEONA HELMSLEY

Leona Helmsley, the woman who made galley slaves out of employees at her string of fancy motels, and told her hired help, "Only the little people pay taxes"—just before she tried to bamboozle the government out of a million smackers. While all of us working stiffs were pinching pennies to pay our fair share of taxes to keep America firing on all cylinders, this porky fatcat was lounging around stuffing her face with caviar and French pastries at our expense. Leona and all of those savings and loan thieves who squandered all our money ought to be locked up for life!

SADDAM HUSSEIN

Saddam Hussein, the towel-headed tyrant that still deserves a little taste of good old American firepower. I'd launch a few jet fighters off the deck of one of those mighty U.S. carriers parked in the Persian Gulf and make a quick, neat job of that sand weasel Hussein. Our top guns could have their breakfast, polish off the butchering bum in minutes, and be back on their flattop for some good Navy chow by lunchtime. That's the same way we dealt with that other tinhorn dictator Muammar Gadhafi. And we haven't heard a peep out of that Libyan loony since U.S. jets gave him a haircut and a trim! I call this pest control.

TEDDY KENNEDY

Teddy Kennedy's a belching, butt-pinching, hungover has-been who had a famous brother and a bunch of relatives with teeth like piano keys. He's a living example for our children of what happens to fat-cat politicians who drink two quarts of scotch whiskey a day and drive off bridges with babes who can't swim. The U.S. Senate without Teddy Kennedy? That would be like Cuba without Castro! Massachusetts oughta change its name from the Bay State to the Brain Damaged State for sending him back to Washington every four years. Terrible Teddy Kennedy is a blubbering sex addict who deserves to be made fun of on T-shirts, billboards, and everything else. Anything to get this bozo out of the Senate, for Pete's sake.
Q. How many Kennedys does it take to change a light bulb?
A. Three. One to hold the bulb and two to drink until the room starts spinning.

JACKIE KENNEDY

Jackie Kennedy was nothing but a rich brat who married another rich brat who happened to become President. She spent most of her time in the White House picking up the bras and panties left lying around by JFK's girlfriends, then learned about three words of Spanish so she could charm the sombreros off a bunch of meathead Mexicans during one of the President's trips back in 1961. What makes me so pig-biting mad is all this weepy, liberal baloney that she was another Dolly Madison or something. This gal Jackie was a phony from the word go. When her husband the President fell off his rocking chair over that, mattress-back actress Monroe, Jackie even started talking in a whisper just like Marilyn, for crying out loud. So let's skip to the bottom line here, my friends: Jackie Bouvier Kennedy Onassis had about as much impact on American history as a fly on an elephant's butt.

"QUOTABLE QUOTES"

"I can't stand Barbra Streisand and I think she knows why."
PRESIDENT RODHAM

"If I ever catch Bill with another woman nobody will remember who Lorena Bobbitt was."
PRESIDENT RODHAM

"If I had a mom like Newt Gingrich's I'd want to bring back the orphanages, too."
PRESIDENT RODHAM

"I may have fat legs, but you try sleeping with Bill Clinton's flabby potbelly."
PRESIDENT RODHAM

SINEAD O'CONNOR

Sinead (what the hell kind of first name is that?) O'Connor, who refused to go onstage at a concert once if they played "The Star Spangled Banner" before the shindig got underway. If this bald-headed bimbo doesn't believe in the Stars and Stripes, then what the hell is she doing over here anyway. Americans everywhere are sick and tired of these showbiz psychos tearing down our greatest tribute to The Land of the Free and the Home of the Brave—our National Anthem.

ROSS PEROT

The guy who couldn't run a washing machine, much less our great country, and the same guy who tried to quit the Navy back in the 1950s because sailors cuss too much! I've seen 'em come and I've seen 'em go—Roosevelt, Truman, Ike, JFK, Johnson, Humphrey, Nixon, Ford, Carter, Reagan, and Bush. This big-eared dingbat from Dallas shouldn't even have his name mentioned in that company, by cracky. The ones I feel sorry for are those poor people who went pie-eyed over the sneaky little money bags, the ones with the gummy car bumpers—from peeling off all those Perot for President stickers!

BART SIMPSON

Bart Simpson, that nasty brat turning American kids into smart-mouthed devils. My grandson Teddy had always been the sweetest, nicest kid you ever saw before that lamebrain TV show came along. "Don't have a cow, Ed," he said to me. As soon as I'm finished with Teddy, I'd be happy to put that Bart Simpson over my knee.

O.J. SIMPSON

Let's face it, folks. O.J. Simpson tried to cut off his wife's head and bumped off that boytoy waiter of hers. Nothing would have made me happier than to see O.J. get executed during halftime of last year's Super Bowl. You heard me right. We could have rolled out a nice big float with an electric chair bolted to it. And those big generators that keep the stadium lights and scoreboards working would provide the juice to zap The Juice. Get it? The fans could have done one of those fancy waves where they stand up and throw their arms in the air, the same way they do after a touchdown. Think of how this added half-time attraction would tear the hearts out of all those screaming, whining, left-wing liberals who want to mollycoddle criminals like O.J.

LIZ TAYLOR

Liz Taylor, that fat Hollywood gal who once almost choked to death trying to swallow a chicken leg. Liz ought to get her mind out of the feedbag and figure out why there's no fella sitting across the table from her—again. After eight husbands she's had more honeymoons than most of us have had vacations! These guys probably don't like sharing the bed with all of her midnight snacks—turkey with all the trimmings, meatball heroes, and big buckets of buttery popcorn, my sources tell me. She's the only actress in Hollywood who takes out insurance on her lunch, owns a double-wide refrigerator, and would fight Arnold "The Terminator" Schwarzenegger to a draw for the last pork chop on the table.

VLADIMIR ZHIRINOVSKY

The Moscow madman who says all patriotic Americans are evil and he wants to have a Star Wars battle with the United States to decide who will rule the world—us or them. So fasten your seat belts, folks. This is going to be the most Cold War fun we've had since Nikita Krushchev banged his shoe on the table at the U.N. more than 30 years ago. Zhirinovsky claims, "Once I control all of Mother Russia, I'll have every guntoting redneck in America wetting their pants." I don't know about you, folks, but them's fighting words to the Anger clan. If we don't reopen all our closed military bases, put our nuclear warhead factories on red alert, bring back the draft, and start cranking out nuclear submarines like rabbits crank out babies, we'll all be speaking Russian before you can say Vladimir Zhirinovsky.

MY OUTBOX
ED ANGER

ED FIRES AWAY!

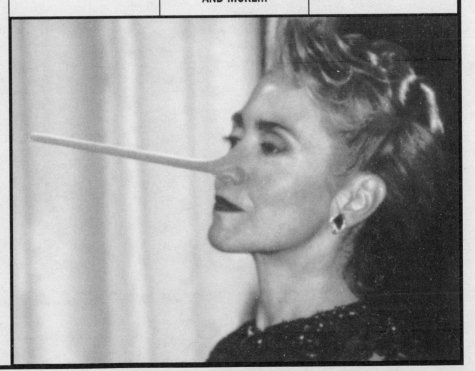

JAPS PULL ANOTHER SNEAK ATTACK!

But we've got a BIG surprise for 'em, says Ed.

Yoshio Sakurauchi, Speaker
House of Representatives (Shugii)
1-7-1 Nagoto-cho Chiyoda-ku
Tokyo 100, Japan

Dear Mr. Sakurauchi,
I've been thinking about what you said about us American workers in the newspaper—that we're lazy, stupid, and will never hold a candle to you Japanese. You said that the United States is nothing more than "Japan's subcontractor" and that you will rule us by the year 2020—just a few years from now.
   You even said you doubted whether idiot American workers would make good slaves for their new Japanese bosses.
   But what got me pig-biting mad, you pinhead rice ball, is when you said Japan's new economic sneak attack on our great country would make Pearl Harbor look like a Sunday school picnic!
   I didn't charge up Pork Chop Hill in Korea back in '52 to let any low-down, conniving, two-faced Jap swindler threaten MY AMERICA 40 years later!
   So I'm gonna put it all on the line, Bubba.
   You said me and my working-stiff buddies made inferior stuff here in the States. Well, I'll tell you one thing that America makes better than anybody else on the planet, mister. The gol-durned atomic bomb, that's what!
   So keep on mouthing off, Mr. Moto. Just remember to take a last look at what's written on the nose cones of the nuclear missiles we're gonna blow the hell out of Tokyo with…
   MADE IN AMERICA, that's what!

Very truly yours,

Ed Anger

Ed Anger

DEAR PREZ CLINTON:
THE ALIEN GOT YOU ELECTED
...NOW GIVE HIM A JOB, SAYS ED!

President Bill Clinton
The White House
Washington, DC

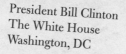

Dear President Clinton:

I knew you would be moving into the White House when the Space Alien jumped on the Clinton-Gore bandwagon.

Let's face it. How the hell could you lose when you had this E.T. telling you everything from how to perk up the economy to showing up Geroge Bush for what he was—a slave to the S&L fatcats who stole us blind in the 1980s.

So I hope you don't forget the spaceman when it comes to filling those high-level NASA posts or even a cabinet position or two. The bottom line, Prez Clinton, is that you owe this lightbulb head big-time and we ain't talkin' about money. You gotta remember, Mr. Prez: The Alien was for Clinton when Clinton wasn't cool!

Yep, when things were looking darkest it was your buddy the Alien who put you on the front page of every darn newspaper in the country—after the *Weekly World News*, of course.

That's when America began to stand up and take notice, Mr. Prez. "If the Space Aliens trust Gov. Clinton then so do I," was the new battle cry that rang out from sea to shining sea.

So here's an Ed Anger salute, sir, to you and your friend from another world. If you guys can't get America back on its feet again, nobody can—including Ross Perot, that Texas tyke-oon!

Ed Anger

NEED I SAY MORE?

ED SENDS OPEN CHALLENGE TO IRAQ'S HUSSEIN:

Let's settle this once and for all... MAN-TO-MAN!

WEEKLY WORLD NEWS

Saddam Hussein
President of the Republic of Iraq
Baghdad
IRAQ

Dear Saddam,

Listen up, you lily-livered camel jockey—if you haven't already been sent on a one-way trip to hell by some brave Marine's M-16 rifle!

Anger's the name and kickin' tail's the game.

That's right, bubba. Let's settle this thing once and for all, just me and you—any-place, anytime.

I'm not the young buck I was when we charged up Pork Chop Hill in Korea back in '52. And I've got a steel plate in my head as a little souvenir from that blood-soaked battlefield.

I even take high blood pressure pills and the old ticker ain't what she used to be. But if I can save the life of one American boy by meeting you face-to-face, man-to-man, on some red hot sand dune, then damn the consequences.

As that late, great American hero John "Duke" Wayne used to say, "I'm gonna finish what you started, Pilgrim, and it ain't going to be a pretty sight."

I've enclosed my unpublished phone number in this envelope, you simpering little sand flea. If you've got the guts, give me a jingle. Let's settle this thing once and for all.

Yours truly,

Ed Anger

Ed Anger

P.S. I just got a call from my travel agent. I've got an open ROUND-TRIP airline ticket to Baghdad. So say the word, you towel-headed tyrant, and I'll be in your face before you can say Saudi Arabia.

ED'S 4TH OF JULY LETTER TO THE FATHER OF OUR COUNTRY!

George Washington
Graveyard
Mt. Vernon, Virginia, 22121

Dear George,

I've gotta tell you that I'm madder than a Redcoat at the Boston Tea Party over what's happened to our great nation since those glorious days when you and the boys put your John Hancocks on the Declaration of Independence and proceeded to whip some British butt.

It took 'em more than 200 years to do it, but a durn bossy woman's our President now. Her name's Hillary Rodham. The American people actually elected her hubby Bill, but he lasted about as long as a bottle of booze in Teddy Kennedy's cabinet—about two minutes.

Hillary wears the pants in the White House now. In fact, I hear they wear the same size pants so they can mix and match, for crying out loud.

Presidential haircuts now cost more than your famous wooden choppers. At $200 a trim, the Clintons would be better off wearing one of your powdered wigs.

And get a load of this, George. The Clintons wanted to have a bunch of people with the weirdest names you ever heard running the government. Folks with names like George Snofolofogus, Zoe (pronounced Zoooo-E) Baird, Kimba (Kimba?) Wood, and Lanie Grand Marnier or something French like that.

If there's one real American name in that lineup, I'll eat my hat.

Most of these people with funny names were dumped, of course, but the country is in deep trouble when they're even considered for White House jobs.

All the Clintons had to do to avoid this name scandal was to look at your White House lineup, George. People with names like Ben, Tom, John, Richard, Jerry, and Andrew.

The only gal's name that popped up on the Washington fast track back then was that late, great seamstress Betsy Lou Ross of American Flag fame.

Nobody named Bambi or Hacienda or Ponderosa—or those hard-to-pronounce Greek names.

But that's the way it is these days, Mr. Washington, and I'm just glad you aren't here to see it.

Your Pal,

Ed Anger

Ed Anger

ED'S LETTER TO NORTH KOREAN BOSS

LET'S GET IT ON!

President Kim Il-Sung
Democratic People's Republic of Korea
c/o North Korean Mission to the U.N.
515 East 72nd Street
New York, NY 10021

Dear Kim:

Okay bubba, I'll get right to the point. We whipped your tails back in '53 and we're about to do it again, by God.

I've lived with a steel plate in my head for 41 years—a little North Korean souvenir from the Battle of Pork Chop Hill.

I lost my best buddy on that bloody day in July, but me and him took out 37 of your crack troops before we went down.

I may be getting a little long in the tooth, but I've still got my Marine uniform hanging in the closet and an M-1 rifle that's oiled and ready to go.

As John "The Duke" Wayne used to say before a gunfight, "Let's dance." Yeah, let's get it on, you crazy Korean.

Our American warplanes will hit you like 10,000 bats out of hell and our fighting men will pour over your borders like banshees. It'll make Armageddon look like a Sunday School picnic.

North Korea will be flatter than a Kmart parking lot when we're through, you buck-toothed, chow mein-gobbling, yellow-bellied coward.

But I've got a way we can avoid all that unpleasantness, Kim, old buddy—and save some innocent lives on both sides.

How about me and you, one on one, weapons of your choice? Winner take all. You win and you can build all the A-bombs you want. I win and North Korea does the whole world's laundry for the next 10 years—by hand.

What say we meet on July 6, the 41st anniversary of Pork Chop Hill, and settle this thing the old-fashioned way—mano on mano?

I'll be waiting to hear from you.

God Bless America,   *Ed Anger*

ED'S LETTER TO THE LATE GREAT BABE RUTH

DEAR BABE: NOW THE SNEAKY JAPS WANNA BUY BASEBALL!

Mr. Babe Ruth
c/o St. Peter
Heaven

Dear Babe,
I know this letter hasn't got a snowball's chance in hell of reaching you, but I had to give it a shot, by gum. I don't know what the headlines in heaven have been saying recently, but the ones on the sports page of my local paper make me sick.

The Japanese are buying a major league ball club, Babe—an American one, for crying out loud. The Seattle Mariners have been sold lock, stock, and dugout to one of those Tokyo bozos who make video games—and Babe, that makes me pig-biting mad.

The next thing you know we'll be singing "Buy me some sushi and blowfish backs," instead of "peanuts and Cracker Jack!"

If we let the Japs buy our national pastime, what next? The Washington Monument and Statue of Liberty?

Whatever happened to the days when the Dodgers were in Brooklyn and you and Lou Gehrig were on Murderers' Row socking homers for sick kids? Hey, who cares if you boozed it up or got involved in some "Yankee Panky" now and then? Those were the days, Babe. America, baseball, and apple pie—and not a buck-toothed riceball in sight.

But it's the Summer of '92, Babe—and a black day for baseball.

The company that bought into the very heart of the American Dream makes Nintendo computer games—including a baseball version that keeps our kids glued to TV screens instead of Little League fields.

And I hate to tell you this, Babe, but a recent survey by Americans for Youth Fitness found that 9 out of 10 boys under the age of 14 have never swung a baseball bat and 7 out of 10 have never played catch!

"Baseball will be more fun when it is played entirely on Nintendo," said one Jap businessman. "Even major league teams in America will soon be reduced to computer chips and little me running in TV screen ballparks. Human players will be obsolete. Ah so!"

Well, Babe, I'm mad as hell and I'm not going to take it anymore.

If baseball is worth saving from this foreign invasion, then every real American will stand up and say, "Let's ban the Japs from every park and God bless the U.S.A!"

Good talking to you, Babe.

Your Pal, *Ed Anger*

ED'S OPEN LETTER TO BORIS YELTSIN—A GOOD OL' RUSSKIE

Boris Yeltsin
The Kremlin
Moscow, Russia

Dear Boris,

I never thought much of you Russkies until I saw you climb up on that tank to stop those coup idiots from taking over the country.

But I got to hand it to you, buddy. That was darned American of you the way you stared 'em down like Gary Cooper in "High Noon." In fact, my personal hero John "Duke" Wayne would've busted his buttons with pride to see you in action.

Let's face it. Some of the lily-livered, yellow-bellied, egg-sucking wimps we call U.S. Congressmen and Senators could learn a thing or two from guys like you.

The boys down at the Dewdrop Bar and Grill heard on TV that you like to take a drink or two. So we decided to put a big bottle of vodka on ice and give you a standing invite to drop by and knock back a couple the next time you're in America.

So here's a snappy Ed Anger salute, Boris. I never thought I'd say this about a Russian, but you've got the most guts of any politician since Harry S. Truman.

And if you ever need any help from an old warhorse, give me a ring. I'll be in Moscow before you can say Mikhail Gorbachev.

Your Pal,

Ed Anger

Ed Anger

YOU'RE MY KIND OF GUY, BORIS!

ANGRY READERS GAVE ME HELL ABOUT DEMI—BUT I'M STILL RIGHT!

I'm madder than a doctor with a dirty golf ball over all the flak I got about the letter I sent Demi Moore. Hey, I told it like it was, for Pete's sake. That picture of her pregnant on the magazine cover was downright disgusting.

Let's face it. Pregnant women ARE ugly.

But did I catch hell from wife Thelma Jean and all the gals in the garden club. They called me every name in the book and some that aren't in anybody's book. And the wife hasn't cooked a hot meal for me since the col-umn came out in *Weekly World News*.

To make things worse, the mailman just dumped about 20,000 letters on my doorstep from furious ladies across America.

Hey, I stand by the column. But everybody's got a right to speak their piece. So here's a little sampling of what you gals out there think about my opinion that pregnant women look like something the cat dragged in:

Dear Pigface: So you hate pregnant women, huh? Well, what do you think that says about your mother? How do you think you were born, fool? If your mother had never gotten pregnant, you wouldn't be here right now writing your hateful filth.—Ann C., Chicago

I had six children and now I am a grandmother and a great grandmother (I'm 92 years young). So, go die, scum!—Agatha C., Toledo

You insufferable fat slob...I wish to hell you could get pregnant and see what it feels like. But you probably already know with that stuffed beer gut, you lard-butt idiot!—Rose D., Niagara Falls, New York

Dear Bone-Brain Ed Anger: Beautiful Demi Moore's got one thing you ain't: Guts! How come you haven't got the courage to publish your own picture. Or maybe you're too damned ugly!—Alice R., Rockford, Illinois

Dear Dumbo: You're so stupid for saying those rotten things about Demi Moore you wouldn't make good slop for my hogs. If I ever meet you, I'm going to rip that steel plate out of your head and pound some sense into you with it.—Evelyn G., San Diego, California

What a total jerk you really are. A pregnant woman's body is the most natural thing on all of God's earth. The motherly swells of Demi's body were absolutely beautiful. Your ignorant opinion only tells me that you don't deserve to be a father. Get a vasectomy!—Thelma C., Manhattan, Kansas

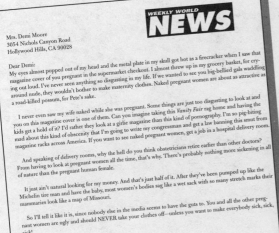

WEEKLY WORLD NEWS

Mrs. Demi Moore
3054 Nichols Canyon Road
Hollywood Hills, CA 90028

Dear Demi:
My eyes almost popped out of my head and the metal plate in my skull got hot as a firecracker when I saw that magazine cover of you pregnant in the supermarket checkout. I almost threw up in my grocery basket, for crying out loud. I've never seen anything so disgusting in my life. If we wanted to see you big-bellied gals waddling around nude, they wouldn't bother to make maternity clothes. Naked pregnant women are about as attractive as a road-killed possum, for Pete's sake.

I never even saw my wife naked while she was pregnant. Some things are just too disgusting to look at and you on this magazine cover is one of them. Can you imagine taking this *Vanity Fair* rag home and having the kids get a hold of it? I'd rather they look at a girlie magazine than this kind of pornography. I'm so pig-biting mad about this kind of obscenity that I'm going to write my congressman and get a law banning this smut from magazine racks across America. If you want to see naked pregnant women, get a job in a hospital delivery room.

And speaking of delivery rooms, why the hell do you think obstetricians retire earlier than other doctors? From having to look at pregnant women all the time, that's why. There's probably nothing more sickening in all of nature than the pregnant human female.

It just ain't natural looking for my money. And that's just half of it. After they've been pumped up like the Michelin tire man and have the baby, most women's bodies sag like a wet sack with so many stretch marks their mammaries look like a map of Missouri.

So I'll tell it like it is, since nobody else in the media seems to have the guts to. You and all the other pregnant women are ugly and should NEVER take your clothes off—unless you want to make everybody sick, sick, sick!

Yours truly,

Ed Anger

Ed Anger

P.S. What the hell kinda name is Demi anyway? Short for Demetrius?

READER MAIL BAG

Aug 25, 1993.

Dear Mr. Anger,

Hello to one of my very favorite columnists. I will say I agree whole heartedly at least 98% of the time with your section in WWN. I just bought the Sept 7, 1993 issue and saw your article about the electric bleachers and I say Go for It. It is high time we got riley that chain on the pocketbook of the decent taxpayers. That would do it. I sent in the signed statement to Pres. Clinton about making Labor Day a real day of rest and retrieve all of the debt except for home mortages, and watch the economy takeoff. then you a lot.

Yours truly,

DEAR PORNO ED,
YOU ARE SUCH AN ANIMAL MALE-FEMALE CHAUVINISTIC PERVERTED MINDED EAST COAST JISSY NEWS TRASH WRITER OR WHATEVER YOU MAY BE.

" I ...I THOUGHT ED AND I ...HAD SOMETHING." SAYS A TEARY-EYED ROSS PEROT AFTER BEING DUMPED ON AN ONE-TIME STAUNCH SUPPORTER, ED ANGER.

we need more thinkers lik you. You sure come up with some good ideas. Wish we could have them all put into effect.

Dixon, Ill. 6/091

SMOKERS HAVE RIGHTS TOO!

START TOMORROW!

☒ YES I AGREE WITH ED ANGER

☐ _____

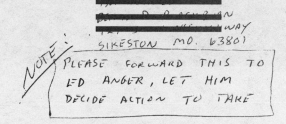

ED ANGER'S THREE-INCOME POLL

YES ☒
America should adopt Ed Anger's plan to allow every man two wives so we can get this great country back on its feet — and to hell with the whiny women's libbers.

NO ☐
We should kowtow to the women's libbers and force men to continue to settle for one wife, even if it means economic collapse and the end of this country as we know it.

Mail your vote to THREE-INCOME POLL, Weekly World News, 600 S. East Coast Ave., Lantana, Fla. 33462

WEEKLY WORLD NEWS August 3, 1993   17

NOTE: SIKESTON MO. 63801

PLEASE FORWARD THIS TO
ED ANGER, LET HIM
DECIDE ACTION TO TAKE

DEAR ED: I WOULD LIKE TO SUGGEST
THAT A SUBJECT OF A FUTURE POLL BE
ON THE SUBJECT "STICKING IT TO THE MILITARY"

YES ☐
NOW THAT THE WORLD IS SUCH A SAFE PLACE, AMERICA
NO LONGER NEEDS A MILITARY SO LETS GIVE THEM
A THANK YOU NOTE AND MARCHING ORDERS BACK TO
CIVILIAN LIFE.

NO ☐
IN MANY WAYS THE WORLD IS A LOT MORE DANGEROUS
NOW THAT THE COLD WAR IS OVER, (SURE IT IS), WE MAY
NEED MILITARY PEOPLE MORE THAN EVER, WE SHOULD
ENCOURAGE YOUNG PEOPLE TO ENTER MILITARY CAR—
WARS of ... ARE FOUGHT WITH ...
"OFF THE SHELF" ...

And furthermore Mr. Anger, what
in your opinion is a Real American
Name? Washington Jefferson, Bush
hickey and Anger all would have sounded
plenty weird to my Ancestors!

Dear Ed:
I don't think you've even given soccer a fair
chance. Soccer is (together with rugby) is one
the roughest, quick thinking, skillful sports
the world. Your pole doesn't give a real "I
.OVE SOCCER" answer; they both say it's
.oring sport. I may be favoring the sport, s
play soccer, but I at least give the sports I
fair chance. If you have any dignity at all
will give soccer another chance, and all
sports you don't particularly like.

I was reading about Foreign Diplom-
ats owing the U.S. Millions in Parking
fines. I agree with Ed. about this.
Blast the damn ties. If
this does not work, tow there cars and
put them in a pond untill they pay

Sincerely,
An angered soccer player,
and team from, Ridgew

THE F.B.I. FILE

This time I'm **PIG-BITING MAD**! My old friend, the late, great J. Edgar Hoover, is spinning in his grave over this FBI file I found under the Freedom of Information Rule, or some **GOLDURNED** thing. I guess this means my sources at the Bureau have been snooping in my garbage all this time, too! They better stay away from my grandson Teddy, or he'll pick them off with his 9-mm Smith and Wesson before they can say "**MOST WANTED**."

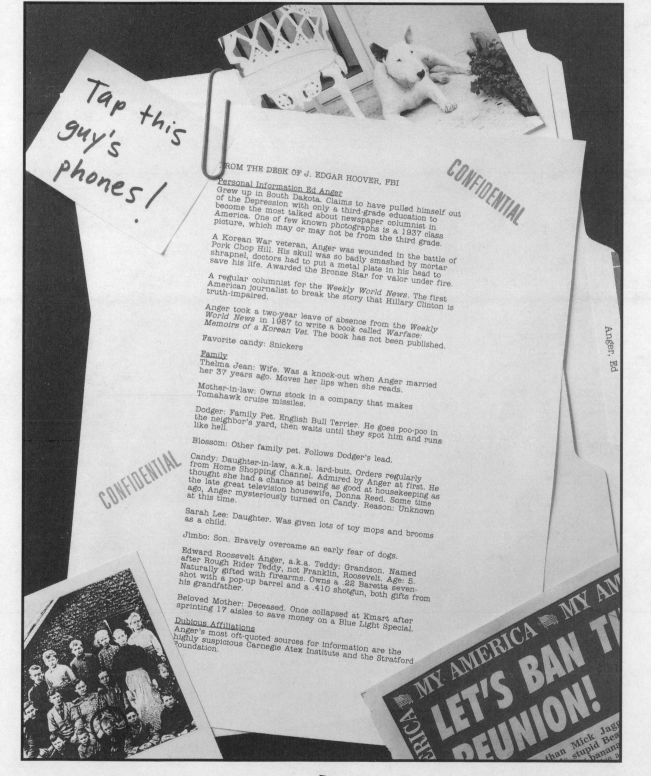

Tap this guy's phones!

FROM THE DESK OF J. EDGAR HOOVER, FBI

CONFIDENTIAL

Anger, Ed

<u>Personal Information Ed Anger</u>
Grew up in South Dakota. Claims to have pulled himself out of the Depression with only a third-grade education to become the most talked about newspaper columnist in America. One of few known photographs is a 1937 class picture, which may or may not be from the third grade.

A Korean War veteran, Anger was wounded in the battle of Pork Chop Hill. His skull was so badly smashed by mortar shrapnel, doctors had to put a metal plate in his head to save his life. Awarded the Bronze Star for valor under fire.

A regular columnist for the *Weekly World News*. The first American journalist to break the story that Hillary Clinton is truth-impaired.

Anger took a two-year leave of absence from the *Weekly World News* in 1987 to write a book called *Warface: Memoirs of a Korean Vet*. The book has not been published.

Favorite candy: Snickers

<u>Family</u>
Thelma Jean: Wife. Was a knock-out when Anger married her 37 years ago. Moves her lips when she reads.

Mother-in-law: Owns stock in a company that makes Tomahawk cruise missiles.

Dodger: Family Pet. English Bull Terrier. He goes poo-poo in the neighbor's yard, then waits until they spot him and runs like hell.

Blossom: Other family pet. Follows Dodger's lead.

Candy: Daughter-in-law, a.k.a. lard-butt. Orders regularly from Home Shopping Channel. Admired by Anger at first. He thought she had a chance at being as good at housekeeping as the late great television housewife, Donna Reed. Some time ago, Anger mysteriously turned on Candy. Reason: Unknown at this time.

Sarah Lee: Daughter. Was given lots of toy mops and brooms as a child.

Jimbo: Son. Bravely overcame an early fear of dogs.

Edward Roosevelt Anger, a.k.a. Teddy: Grandson. Named after Rough Rider Teddy, not Franklin, Roosevelt. Age: 5. Naturally gifted with firearms. Owns a .22 Baretta seven-shot with a pop-up barrel and a .410 shotgun, both gifts from his grandfather.

Beloved Mother: Deceased. Once collapsed at Kmart after sprinting 17 aisles to save money on a Blue Light Special.

<u>Dubious Affiliations</u>
Anger's most oft-quoted sources for information are the highly suspicious Carnegie Atex Institute and the Stratford Foundation.

CONFIDENTIAL

MY AMERICA ≋ MY AM
ERICA ≋ MY AMERICA

**LET'S BAN TH
REUNION!**

than Mick Jagg
stupid Bea
banan